D1106288

ANDREW CARNEGIE AND THE AGE OF STEEL

ANDREW CARNEGIE

AND THE AGE OF STEEL

BY KATHERINE B. SHIPPEN

Illustrated with photographs

and with drawings by ERNEST KURT BARTH

RANDOM HOUSE • NEW YORK

 Published in New York by Random House, Inc., and simultaneously in Toronto, Canada, by Random House of Canada, Limited.

Library of Congress Catalog Card Number: 58–6179
Manufactured in the United States of America

CONTENTS

ANDREW CARNEGIE AND THE AGE OF STEEL

1

DUNFERMLINE AND A WEAVER'S SON

On the other side of the ocean, in the village of Dunfermline in Scotland, Andrew Carnegie, home from school on a winter afternoon, sat beside his father at the loom. He was ten years old in 1847. That was the year the iron ore mines were discovered north of Lake Superior. But Andrew had never heard of that.

He liked school well enough: Mr. Marten, his teacher, sat on a high platform, his hat on the desk beside him. But better than school Andrew liked to sit with his father at the loom. Often the two of them sang together while the loom clicked, and there was scarcely an old Scottish song that they did not know. The boy with white hair and blue eyes, though he was small for his age, had a good strong voice. He opened his mouth wide when he sang; and his voice, mingled with his father's deeper tones, went echoing through the workshop.

One of the ballads they liked best to sing was about a Scotsman who had been exiled in India.

The palm tree waveth high, and fair the myrtle springs
And to the Indian maid the bulbul sweetly sings;
But I dinna see the broom wi' its tassels on the lea,
Nor hear the linties' sang o' my ain countrie.

Andrew's father, Will, wore shirt sleeves at his work and a long white apron; for he was weaving tablecloths of linen damask, and everything must be scrupulously clean. The weaver's hands worked in rhythm to the song, knocking the shuttle from right to left, and his feet worked the treadles as the pattern grew. Sometimes Andrew saw figures of birds or of roses. There were beautiful scrolls worked into some of the tablecloths, and occasionally his father made grand coats of arms.

The house where the Carnegies lived had only two rooms. His mother Margaret and his father Will, Andrew and his young brother, Tom, all slept and ate their meals in the room upstairs. The downstairs room was the workshop where his father kept his looms.

Andrew's mother used to spin the linen thread for the weaving. He liked to watch her as she worked—her black hair combed back from her pale face, and she sitting up so straight. As she finished each reel of linen thread, she carried it across the room and put it into his father's tall hat which stood on the table beside him. That was the same hat that, emptied of its reels, Andrew's father put on his head to wear to church each Sunday.

Sometimes the boy grew tired of sitting still. Then he would run over to his Uncle Lauder's place. Uncle Lauder kept the greengrocer's shop in the High Street, and he was an important man. When Uncle Lauder went outdoors, he wore a long brown cape that reached to his knees, and his head was topped with a tall silk hat. But when he was in the shop, you could see that his hair was light brown and silky. His deep gray eyes were quiet and rather wistful as he stood among his barrels of whitings and salt herring, his sacks of onions and potatoes.

What Andrew learned from Uncle Lauder was a passionate love of Scotland. To walk with him through the Scottish woods with their bluebells and over the Scottish moors with their heather; to recite the lyrics of Robert

Burns and the epics of Sir Walter Scott; to dream of the bravery of Sir William Wallace, the stout Scottish hero, and of Robert Bruce, who was Scotland's first king, was part of what he taught him. Every stone in Dunfermline Abbey held interest for Uncle Lauder, and he never tired of telling of the kings and queens who had once walked there.

"Uncle Lauder." Andrew came running into the grocery shop one day, hardly pausing long enough to give Uncle Lauder good day. "A boy in school said England was bigger than Scotland!"

Andrew looked at Uncle Lauder for help, for he was angry and worried that anyone should say such a thing.

Uncle Lauder had been measuring out sugar from a barrel at the back of his shop. He looked at Andrew a moment, considering his answer.

"Well, lad," he said, "if Scotland was rolled out flat, it would be bigger than England—but who ever would want Scotland to be flat?"

So it was all right; Andrew understood Scotland was the way it ought to be.

There was another annoying day when the same annoying boy had tried to tell Andrew that England had more people in it than Scotland.

"But the English outnumbered the Scotch more than eight to one at the Battle of Bannockburn, and still we beat them," Uncle Lauder said.

It was always that way with Uncle Lauder. There was never any doubt about the greatness of Scotland.

One night Andrew stayed longer than usual at Uncle Lauder's. It was beginning to grow dark as he ran down the street toward home. The light of the lamps shone out from the windows of the weavers' cottages. He reached his own house and pushed open the door. The lamp was already lighted, and he saw his mother and father with little Tom, and his Aunt Kitty and Aunt Anne and Uncle Hogan, all standing round the table looking down at a map.

"That's Pennsylvania," his Uncle Hogan was saying. "There's Pittsburgh. . . . It'll be a long journey even after we get to America."

So, it turned out, his two aunts and his uncle were going to America. But why should anyone want to leave Scotland, Andrew wondered. He thought and thought about it, but he could not imagine.

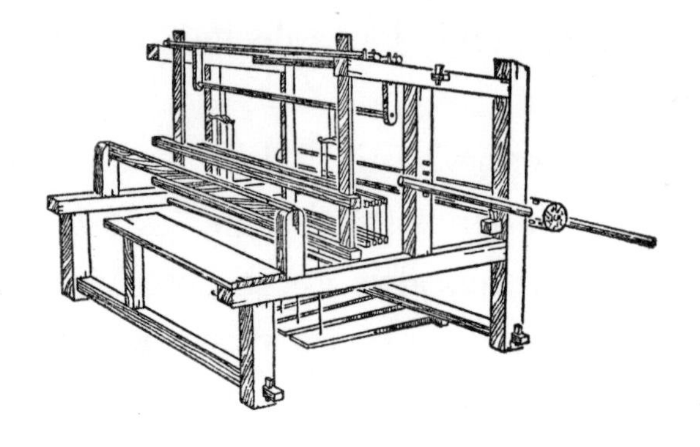

2

POVERTY AND A DECISION

Why should anyone ever want to leave Dunfermline? Kings and queens had walked where now the weavers and their families lived and worked. The thought of them gave pride to every boy in the village. This was the very heart of Scotland. The walls of the palace

Robert Bruce had built were still standing. The roof of it was gone, but you could see the oriole windows in the walls. And the bones of Robert Bruce lay in the Abbey Church. Outside the village, in the bluebell-carpeted glen, you could see the cave where Sir William Wallace hid from his enemies.

But changes came to Dunfermline. And Andrew's family and many other families had a bitter choice to make. Along the streets where the weavers lived, the clicking of almost all the looms grew quiet. And at the edge of the town a shed housed twenty looms driven by steam power. They worked faster than the old hand looms, and it took no special skill to operate them. "But I don't believe they can make patterns of birds and flowers," Andrew said loyally.

Then a day came when the boy's father came in saying, "Andra, I canna get nae more work." The steam-powered looms were the reason, he explained to the boy. All sorts of people—men, women and children—worked at the steam-powered looms. They did not sell the things they made but worked for wages. They did not own the looms they worked on, nor decide what they should make nor how they should work. They came to the factory early in the morning and worked till dark, so they never saw their homes in the daytime. And the cloth they wove was of poor quality—but it was cheap.

The weavers in Andrew's street and all through the town were indignant and fearful when they saw the factory working. Of course these machines could turn cloth out faster, but it was no good, they said. Of course the factory owners could sell it cheaper—they paid out so little in wages.

It had been the weavers' custom in Dunfermline to stop the looms every day at noon while the men went into the street to smoke a pipe and talk together; and they continued to do it, even when they had no work. Generally one of them read aloud from a newspaper. But now they forgot the affairs of the outside world, for Dunfermline had cares of its own. What could be done about the steam-powered looms? Every weaver agreed that it was getting harder and harder to sell the handwoven fabrics that took so many hours to make. Yet there was not one of them that was willing to work in the factory. One of Andrew's uncles suggested that they might go in a body and wreck the factory —but the others were not willing to agree to this.

So when the noon hour was over—spent in talk—they went back into their houses again.

Andrew's father was one of the first to sell his looms. He loved them, but what was the use of making handwoven damask tablecloths? No one would buy them.

His mother tried opening a little greengrocer's shop where she sold onions, turnips and potatoes and "pokes o' sweeties" for the children, but business was poor. Hardly any of the weavers had any money to spend. In the evenings she tried to make a little money binding shoes. Andrew used to sit beside her to thread the needles because he had such good eyes.

Then one day a letter came from America. Andrew's aunts and uncle wanted them to come to Pennsylvania. "Things are much better over here," his aunt wrote.

No doubt it would be better to try America, the Carnegies decided after reading the letter. Will Carnegie had done his best, but the factories made the weaver's trade impossible. His weaving did not bring in nearly enough. Surely it would be better to go.

But the passage to America was expensive, and the Carnegies' savings had been eaten away. How could they pay passage for four across the ocean? Their looms, which had been their dearest possessions, had been sold and the money spent.

"We could put our furniture up at auction,"

Andrew's mother said. "Likely it would bring enough."

So the auctioneer came, and the sale was held. But when it was over and the people had gone away, they counted the money—and there was not enough.

Not far from the Carnegies' house, their old friends, the Fargies, kept a bakery shop. It was Ailie Fargie who came to them now.

"I have some money," Ailie Fargie said. "It's money I put away now and again from the bakery. With what you have from the sale it would be enough. Take it. You can send it back to me sometime."

Years after Andrew remembered his mother's expression and the little moment of silence in the room.

"I'll take it, Ailie Fargie," his mother said. "We'll send it back to ye."

3

"A GOOD STURDY VESSEL"

The last things Andrew saw, as the omnibus carried them slowly down the road in the direction of Glasgow, were the towers of the Abbey Church where Robert Bruce lay buried. He watched them quietly as they grew smaller;

then suddenly without any warning he burst into tears.

"There, Andra." His mother drew him over toward her on the omnibus seat. He was twelve years old, too big to cry.

His father and Tommy rode along in silence, not looking back. His two uncles and his Cousin Doddy, who were going as far as Glasgow to see them off, did not notice his tears.

The journey was over at last, and they climbed down from the omnibus and walked across the cobbled street to the wharf where their ship was tied. She was named the *Wiscasset* and had been built as a whaling ship in the state of Maine. But the whaling ship had been converted to a square-rigger to carry passengers, for the immigrant trade was profitable in the middle of the nineteenth century.

"A good sturdy vessel," Andrew's father said, trying to reassure his family as they stood huddled together on the deck with the other passengers and the sailors milling around them. The *Wiscasset* looked very small to them when they thought of the miles of ocean she had to cross.

"Ay, a good sturdy ship," Andrew's Uncle Lauder repeated. He was very dignified in his frock coat, top hat and good stout walking stick. It seemed as if he knew everything about ships.

But now as the minutes passed and the moment of departure approached, neither Andrew's father nor Uncle Lauder nor any of the rest of them could find anything more to say.

At length there was a great blast on a horn and cries of "All ashore that's going ashore." Uncle Lauder and Uncle Tommy kissed Mrs. Carnegie, who stood erect and rather stiff with her shawl drawn around her. They grasped her husband by the hand and turned toward the boys. But the tears flooded down into Andrew's eyes again, and he hid his face in the folds of Uncle Lauder's frock coat.

"I canna leave ye. I canna leave ye," he sobbed. A kindly sailor drew the boy away. And Uncle Lauder with his Uncle Tommy and his Cousin Doddy—all were gone with the other visitors. The ship was loose from its moorings, and she was floating down the Clyde toward the sea.

That evening they passed the point of rock called Ailsa Craig. It was the last bit of land they were to see for more than six weeks.

Even the most homesick boy can forget his sorrows when he hears the waves slapping against the bow of a ship and feels the salt wind blowing in his face. Soon his skin had been burned brown with sun and salt spray, and his towhead bleached whiter still with the sun.

The Carnegies slept like the other passengers in bunks down in the vessel's hold, but all day long they stayed on deck. There Mrs. Carnegie cooked the food they had brought with them. There was a little stove on the deck. Andrew did odd jobs for the ship's master, coiling the ropes and swabbing the decks with salt water that had a little vinegar in it.

After they had been at sea about a week a northeast storm struck. The sailors went racing up and down the masts to furl the sails while the great waves washed across the deck. Then the Carnegies with the other passengers were ordered below deck, and the hatches were battened down. They rode the storm out sitting on their bunks, the smoky whale-oil lantern swinging back and forth as the vessel rocked. There was no chance to cook any hot food. They ate cheese and hard bread and waited. They were too sick to want to eat anyway.

After a day and a night the storm cleared. The passengers were allowed on deck again but walked carefully, for the vessel was swinging in the trough of the sea.

So day after day they moved on across the ocean, marveling at the dreamy stars at night and the mists that blew across their bows by day. Once, off the starboard bow they saw a towering iceberg that glittered with a mysterious shining as their vessel came near it.

"There's much more of that iceberg underwater than above it," one of the sailors told Andrew and Tommy, who stood at the railing to watch the gleaming mass of ice.

Sometimes a school of porpoises went flipping along, chasing each other through the waves; and once a sailor showed them the shining spout of water that a whale sent up. But it was far off, almost at the horizon—they could not see the whale.

Often in the evenings during the long twilight before night came down, Andrew and his father used to sit and listen to the talk of the passengers—talk of New York and Boston and Chicago—talk of the new world that none of them knew much about.

"And where will you be going, Mr. Carnegie?" they asked Andrew's father—and he told them Pittsburgh, and that he had relatives there already.

"It's a tidy distance to Pittsburgh, I've heard," one of the men said. "Will ye go by stagecoach?"

But Andrew's father told them he had been advised to take a steamboat up the river and then change over to the Erie Canal.

What would it all be like, Andrew wondered as he listened to their talk. Would there be hills like the heather-covered bens in Scotland? What would he do in this new world that lay unseen beyond the edge of the horizon?

Next day there were gray sea gulls flying along over the wake of their ship, and toward evening the passengers were crowding over to the rail, straining their eyes at a thin, dark line on the horizon.

"It's America!" everybody was saying. For every one of them the word had a different meaning. And none of them really knew what it would be like.

4

A SAILOR AND SOME SARSAPARILLA

"Ye can look around if you've a mind to," Andrew's father said. "Your mother and Tommy will sit here with the bags. I'll go down to arrange passage with the river steamer."

The *Wiscasset* had docked after her long voyage. It was June in the year 1848.

The Carnegies had walked down the gang-plank and were standing on the sea wall looking out over the busy waters of New York harbor.

"Here's a bench," Andrew's father said. "Help me get these bundles over to it, Andrew."

Soon Andrew's mother and Tommy were seated there watching the ships in the harbor, while his father had disappeared into a door marked "Hudson River Steamers," and Andrew was free to explore.

Everything was bright and lively that spring morning—Andrew's first day in America. Men and women, elegantly dressed, were walking along the promenade beside the water. Carts loaded with barrels and sacks were rattling over the cobblestones. Newcomers, like the Carnegies themselves, were struggling along with bags and bundles. Andrew stopped to watch a Negro who was selling peanuts—the first Negro he had ever seen. As he was standing absorbed in what was to him a great curiosity, an omnibus came by. Its plunging horses nearly knocked him over before he pulled himself back out of the way.

"Things move around quicker in America," he thought to himself, admiringly.

He had come now to a little booth over which a sign was lettered: "Sarsaparilla, Five Cents." An Irish woman in a big checked apron was pouring the foamy brown liquid into brown china mugs with handles. Andrew pushed up close in the little knot of people around the stand.

"Want to try it, sonny?" A tall, red-faced sailor at his elbow reached across and put down a five-cent piece on the counter.

"Sarsaparilla for the young man," he said.

The woman in the gingham apron pushed a foaming mug toward him. Andrew reached out and took it and began to drink. It was cool and bubbly and had a kind of sweet flavor he had never tried before.

He took another gulp, letting the sparkly

stuff flow down his throat. Then he turned to the sailor. But he had disappeared. Andrew could not see him anywhere in the crowd. He turned back to his mug and finished his drink slowly.

"America must be a good country," he said to himself. "A strange sailor to give a boy a drink that costs five cents. Someday I'll find him again and pay him back."

But he never could, though he tried.

5

A NEWCOMER LOOKS AT THE HUDSON

Andrew reached the place where he had left his mother and Tommy with the pleasant sensation of the sarsaparilla still in his throat. His father had just returned from the steamboat office.

"I got the passage," he was saying. "A bargain too—only a dollar apiece to Albany! They'll be starting in ten minutes."

He picked up the biggest of their bags, Andrew and Tommy each took others, and they made their way to the wharf where a group of passengers were already waiting.

They looked curiously at the boat that would take them up the river.

"She's not very good to look at." Andrew's father was talking to one of his fellow passengers while they waited at the gate. The man wore a checked vest and a heavy gold watch chain and seemed well acquainted with the ways of the world.

"A clumsy-looking boat, they'd say on the Clyde."

"But she's comfortable for traveling," the man answered. "She makes the trip to Albany twice a week. . . ."

The man would have gone on with his praise

of river travel, but a horn blew and the passengers were moving through the gate.

The boat was pleasant enough when you got on board her. She had a big dining room, a deck cabin for ladies, staterooms, a reading room, and besides all this, a promenade deck protected by a striped awning, with comfortable seats where you could sit and watch the scenery go by.

It was not long before they had left the houses of the city behind them and were gliding up the river trailing a plume of smoke.

It was a sunny spring morning, and there was a brisk wind that stirred the surface of the water and raised it into little white-capped waves. Sea gulls came swirling and sweeping around them. You could see the soft feathers of their under parts, their black eyes and coral feet.

There were not many houses along the river banks, but green trees grew right down to the water's edge. Sometimes the boat came close to the shore, and you could see a man fishing or a deer with upstanding ears looking across the water.

All the passengers were talking about the river as they went along it.

"There's been a lot of history along her shores," Andrew heard one of them say. "Over there on the left is where Aaron Burr shot Alexander Hamilton."

"Ay, and that's where George Washington ferried his troops across from Manhattan to New Jersey," another said.

But to Andrew standing up at the front of the boat watching the gulls sweep back and forth, these things meant very little. For he knew of the exploits of William Wallace and the Bruce and, though Uncle Lauder had told him something about George Washington, his name meant little to the white-haired Scottish boy who was beginning to be an American.

The river itself and not its history was what

held his attention. On its left bank the shore was rising in a great beautiful wall of stone.

"It's the Palisades," someone said. "It stretches twenty miles."

And then the stream broadened out into a wide bay, and the boat made its way across the bay, and the river went on winding among sharp pointed hills.

"They are like the Scottish highlands," Andrew thought. "But the bens in Scotland are purple with the heather—and these are green."

He saw the brickyards right down near the shore at Haverstraw, and someone showed him West Point like a fort high above the river.

So they glided on and on up the great river, and morning changed to afternoon and afternoon to supper time, but they did not go into the big dining room since they wanted to save their money. They had brought some bread and cheese with them in their bag.

At a place called Catskill some richly dressed

people got off. They were going to spend the summer in the mountains. That was what a great many rich people in America did, Andrew learned.

And so the steamboat moved on quietly into the dark, and Andrew and his family sat dozing and nodding with their bags beside them. There were streaks of light in the sky when the motion of the boat stopped, and they heard excitement and commotion around them.

They were in Albany. The first part of the long American journey was finished. The passengers scattered.

"Strange," Andrew thought, "I'll not see any of them again. But they are part of America and so am I."

6

"AMERICA MUST BE BIG?"

"What will the Erie Canal be like?" Andrew asked his father. For they were to travel by canal on the last leg of their journey.

"I couldna tell ye, lad," Andrew's father answered. "I dinna know at all." There were too many strange things in this new country: the weaver from Dunfermline could not be expected to understand them all.

They were walking through the noisy streets of Albany with a group of other people who had booked passage in the canal boat.

"I can tell you." A tall man in a beaver hat and heavy gold watch chain was walking near them, and he had heard Andrew's question.

"I've traveled on it often." Andrew looked up at the speaker who seemed to be very much a man of the world. "It's like a big ditch," he said. "A ditch that's forty feet wide. And it goes right across New York State–right over the hills and through the valleys till it gets to Lake Erie."

Andrew was silent, but he thought about what the man had said as he tugged his bag along. How could the ditch that was forty feet wide manage to cross the hills, he wondered. Why didn't all the water flow out of it when they tried to make it go uphill?

Most of the other passengers were there already when they reached the place where the canal boat was moored.

"She looks something like Noah's ark," Andrew thought. For the boat was broad, low, and stubby at both ends. And it had a kind of a low house set in the middle of the deck. This house had a row of little windows which were open now so that the red curtains flapped in the wind.

Inside the house there was a big room, a little room marked "Ladies' Cabin," and a kitchen presided over by a Negro cook. The big room was for sitting in if there was a storm, for eating in at mealtimes, and for sleeping in at night.

"They make up the beds at night in three tiers. If there are too many men to fit into them, they sleep on the dining room table or on the floor. . . . First come first served. The ladies, of course, sleep in the Ladies' Cabin."

The talkative passenger laughed.

But Andrew and his family did not linger in

the cabin, nor waste their sympathies on the unfortunates who had come too late to reserve a place to sleep. They hurried up the steep steps to the roof of the little house and sat there with some of the other passengers to see what was going on.

They did not have to wait long. A boy was leading three horses up along the towpath at the edge of the canal. He harnessed them one behind the other and tied the traces to a long, thick rope that was attached to the canal boat. Then there was a loud blast on the captain's horn; the horses strained and pulled at their traces; and very slowly the boat began to move.

It was a gentle, pleasant movement as the three horses pulled the clumsy boat along the canal. The travelers saw a farmer cutting hay in the warm June meadow and a group of cattle standing close together in the shade of a great tree. Once, two little girls in blue dresses came running out of a farmhouse to wave to them as they went by. And again they passed a small boy in a wide-brimmed hat who was trying to fish in the canal.

Every now and then their boat passed under a bridge. "Low bridge! Low bridge!" the boatman would shout then, and everybody would get up and rush helter-skelter down the stairs to the cabin, to wait till they had passed the bridge.

Some of the passengers whiled away the time by playing cards as the boat moved along. One lady was doing embroidery, and another was reading. But most of them sat talking or looking out across the meadows and planning what they would do when they reached their journey's end.

As time passed, some of the passengers grew tired of sitting still. They jumped over to the towpath when the boat rubbed close to the shore and ran along beside the horses. Andrew wanted to go with them.

"But you might fall into the water," his mother said when he proposed it. "Better sit still."

It was mid-afternoon when they came to their first lock, and Andrew found out how a canal boat could cross a hill.

There was a great hooting and tooting by the boatman as they approached the lock. A man ran out of a little house close to the tow-path and began grinding a handle which closed a pair of heavy gates right across the canal. They were tight shut by the time the canal boat reached the lock, the horses were un-harnessed, and the boat was enclosed as in a snug box. Now a gate was closed behind the boat, and water came pouring down so that the level of the water rose. At last the boat had risen to the upper level, the gates ahead opened, fresh horses were hitched to the boat, and it went gliding out along the canal again.

"So that's a lock," Andrew thought. "And that's the way a canal boat can go uphill."

Day after day the Carnegies traveled thus, with bridges and locks now and again, and twice a day fresh horses to pull them. Day after day they looked out across the fresh June meadows and saw the sun go down, and saw the stars come out at night. Sometimes they went gliding along in the moonlight, and the moonlight was so bright that they could see the shadows of trees and bushes as they passed.

At Buffalo the Erie Canal ended, and they transferred to another canal that took them down into Pennsylvania. Day after day they traveled, and the farms around them seemed always the same.

"America must be big," Andrew was thinking, "for we have traveled more than three weeks, and we haven't come to the end of it yet." He made up his mind to write to Uncle Lauder and tell him how big America was.

At Pittsburgh Andrew's two aunts and his Uncle Hogan were waiting for them, to take them home.

7

THE BOBBIN BOY

The voyage by land and by sea had taken the Carnegies nearly three months, and now it was ended. They had reached Allegheny across the river from Pittsburgh. It was a rough, primitive town. People said it was celebrated for its mud, for its frequent floods and its epidemics of cholera.

The house where Aunt Anne and Aunt Kitty and Uncle Hogan lived was in a ramshackle district along the river bank, a shabby house that needed paint. Yet though they were poor (one of the aunts had a little grocery and Uncle Hogan was a clerk in a crockery shop), they had made such preparations as they could for the Carnegies' coming.

Across the alley there was a rickety shed with a loom which Uncle Hogan had used when he first came to America. In this shed the newcomers settled down, unpacking such small things as they had brought from home. And here Andrew's father began to work at the loom again. He made checked tablecloths this time which he tried rather unsuccessfully to peddle from door to door.

There seemed to be even less market for handwoven stuff in Pennsylvania than there had been in Dunfermline. He tried working in a factory for a time, but he couldn't get used to this strange kind of work and went back to his loom again.

That was why Andrew's mother, having sent little Tom to school, set herself to binding shoes as she had done in Scotland. And that was why Andrew, although he was only twelve, set about looking for work.

He found work after a short time—the Blackstock Cotton Mill needed a bobbin boy. That meant tending the machine that reeled the thread on spools.

"It will pay me $1.20 a week," he told his mother and father, thinking the amount seemed larger because it would be paid in American money. The hours were from six in the morning till six o'clock at night.

The new bobbin boy worked diligently, and before very long the manager sent for him to say that he would be advanced. Now his pay would be $1.65 a week, and the additional forty-five cents was very welcome in the Carnegie family.

"It's in the basement," Andrew told them. "I have to tend the engine and the boiler." That was a great responsibility for a twelve-year-old boy. "Sometimes I'm worried," he told his mother. "If I put on too much coal, the boiler might burst. If I let the fire go down too far, the men will call down that they haven't got enough power."

"Do it the best you can," Margaret Carnegie said, wishing that her boy could go to school instead.

But now another task was added to Andrew's job. He must take the finished bobbins that were sent down to him and dip them in a vat of oil. The oil was sticky and evil-smelling, and it stuck to his hands and could not be washed off. Soon his clothes and hair were filled with the smell. It was the smell that was the horror to him. Working there in the basement day after day he was conscious only of the nauseating smell. He never thought of giving up the job. William Wallace would not have given it up he knew. But day after day he went home weak and sick with the smell of the oil, and at night he woke from dreams of the steam gauges, to smell the evil odor of the oil again.

Now Uncle Lauder and his Cousin Doddy and the boys in Mr. Marten's school seemed far away from him, and he missed the click of his father's loom and the singing. But he kept on.

One night he was walking home to Rebecca Street when he met a group of boys about his own age standing at the street corner.

The boys stared at the short, blue-eyed stranger with his white hair and the foreign cut to his clothes.

"Scotchie," one of them said.

And then they all began to shout at him. "Scotchie! Scotchie!" they shouted in derision.

Andrew stopped and drew himself up as tall as he could.

"I am a Scotsman," he shouted back. "Ay, I

am a Scotchie, and I'm prood o' the name!"

But even as he stood there, with the sob in his throat, he knew that he was no longer really a Scotsman. He was beginning to be an American. And it was hard.

8

"TAKE CARE OF YOURSELF, LADDIE"

Uncle Hogan liked to play checkers. It was this fact that brought an unexpected change in Andrew's fortunes. For, one day Uncle Hogan was sitting, pipe in hand, over the checkerboard with his friend David Brooks, and Mr. Brooks asked him if he knew of a likely boy to carry telegraph messages.

Mr. Brooks was the manager of the Pittsburgh telegraph office. The telegraph was a new thing in America then. Samuel F. B. Morse had invented it only about ten years before, and people were still marveling at the mysterious poles and wires. Prosperous businessmen considered it quite the thing to transact their business by wire, and boys were needed to carry messages from the telegraph office to their offices.

Did Uncle Hogan know of a likely boy to carry messages?

Of course he did. He forgot his Scottish reserve in describing the intelligence and industry of young Andrew. And finally he agreed to have Andrew come to see Mr. Brooks next morning.

Andrew's father was doubtful about having his son apply for the new job. "Better let well enough alone," he said. Mr. Brooks would pay

$2.50 a week to have the new boy—but surely if he paid so much he would want a stronger boy and a bigger one. Anyway, maybe there would be calls at night; perhaps the work would lead the boy into bad company.

But Andrew's mother saw in the new employment a release from the cellar where he had been working, and Andrew himself rejoiced to think that he would escape from the terrible smell of oil. There was no doubt in either of their minds.

Early next morning mother and son began their preparations for the interview with Mr. Brooks. Andrew scrubbed with soap and water till his pink face shone, and brushed his pale hair till it glistened. He had only one change of clothing—the clothes he wore to church on Sundays—and these they decided were required for the occasion. So he put on the white linen shirt that his mother had washed and ironed for him, his blue flannel pants and jacket. And mother, father and son felt there was little to be desired in his appearance as he started for the interview.

Andrew's father went with him: they walked together in the bright sunshine over the bridge to Pittsburgh. But on the way Andrew explained that he would like to talk to Mr. Brooks alone, and his father agreed. He would wait at the corner of Wood and Fourth Streets. The boy was not to promise more than he could do.

Mr. Brooks was a kindly man. After his first embarrassment, Andrew was not afraid. He explained that although he was short and small, he would like very much to try to be a telegraph boy. He did not know the names of the Pittsburgh streets very well, but he was sure he could memorize them.

"When could you begin?" Mr. Brooks asked him after a while.

Andrew looked at him with round blue eyes. "Right away," he said.

It took only a minute to rush downstairs to tell his father the news.

"Take care of yourself, laddie," his father said. He started at once to bear the news back to his wife and Uncle Hogan while Andrew went to start his new job.

Back in the office where everything was clean and sunny and businesslike, Andrew, in a world of pencils, envelopes and telegraph blanks, drew a deep quiet breath of triumph.

"I want you to know the other telegraph boy," Mr. Brooks said—he had but one other. So he called in George McLain.

"George, you must show Andrew how to go about the work," Mr. Brooks said. "It will take him a day or so to learn."

George McLain looked Andrew up and down—the smoothly brushed white hair, the pink face, the neat blue flannel suit.

"I don't know what you're going to do with such a *little* boy," he said.

Andrew winced but said nothing.

9

THREE DOLLARS A WEEK!

Freed now from the dark basement, released from the evil smell of oil, and forgetful of the steam gauges, Andrew, the telegraph boy, took up his new work. He was fourteen years old now; and, though he was still so small, he soon outdid the critical George McLain.

So he ran back and forth in the Pittsburgh streets and darted in and out of doorways and up and down flights of steps. Important businessmen looked up from their desks when the fair-haired boy appeared with messages and recognized him when they passed him in the streets. Sometimes he met them on the sidewalks and delivered his "wire" to them there.

Before many days passed, he could recite the name of every important business firm in the city and tell where its office was located. He was proud of this accomplishment, for it meant that no time was lost in searching for addresses.

He had not been working long when a telegraph line was put through to the eastern seaboard. That meant that messages came pouring into Pittsburgh faster than ever.

"We'll need another boy," Mr. Brooks said one morning. And the next week still a fourth was needed. Before long there were five of them.

One day, not long after the fifth boy was

engaged, James D. Reid, the superintendent, visited the office. Andrew liked him, for he had been born in Dunfermline. All five of the telegraph messengers stood in a row to be inspected the first day Mr. Reid came to the offices. They all looked very neat with clean white collars and well polished shoes.

"They're nice looking lads," Mr. Reid said. "But they'd look lots better if their clothes matched. Why shouldn't they wear uniforms?"

Uniforms were not so common then as now. But the superintendent sent all five boys to a good tailor and ordered jackets and knickerbockers of forest green.

The boys were very proud of their new green suits, and they went in a body to thank Mr. Reid. When they knocked on his door and he called for them to come in, they entered and stood in a self-conscious little row to be inspected. They had chosen Andrew to make the speech of thanks. So the busy days passed.

One day a message was given Andrew to take

to the manager of the Pittsburgh Theater. The manager liked Andrew and told him that if he would wait a little while the play would begin. So Andrew climbed up to the top gallery and sat down. It was kind of the manager, Andrew thought, for a seat up there cost twenty-five cents. He had never been in a theater before that night, and his blue eyes stared when he saw the rose-colored boxes, the seats covered with pink velvet, the gold-embroidered draperies, the crystal chandeliers. Finally, when the great velvet curtain rose, he saw the men and women on the stage and heard the words of Shakespeare on their lips.

Back in Dunfermline, Uncle Lauder had taught him the poetry of Robert Burns, and he never doubted that the Scottish poet was the greatest poet in the world. But here, now, sitting in his green uniform in the poorest seat of the Pittsburgh Theater, he heard the lines of a Shakespearean play, and knew there was another poet besides Robert Burns.

The manager of the theater got a great many telegrams and, after that night, Andrew tried to deliver them all in the evening while the plays were on.

So the days passed, and America appeared a different kind of place from the one he had seen from the Erie Canal boat. It was a lively place of business by day, a place of warmly lighted drama and poetry at night. It was a place where a boy who worked hard was recognized, and where his work was rewarded with money that he could carry home in his pocket.

Andrew earned three dollars a week now. It seemed to him a great sum. Every Saturday he carried it home to his mother. She put it with the four dollars she earned herself binding shoes, and to the occasional sum his father brought when he sold a tablecloth. The money, taken all together, paid rent and bought food for the family, and shoes and clothes for all four of them. Little Tom was still at school, but Andrew was proud because he was almost a man now and could contribute to the family expenses.

Every Saturday night when he brought home the money he had earned, Andrew saw his mother take some coins and put them away in a stocking which she kept in a drawer. As time passed, the stocking grew heavier until after a while there was a hundred dollars in it.

"Take this and go to the post office," his mother said, "and buy a money order for Ailie Fargie. She won't have to wait any longer to have her savings back."

That night there was warmth and contentment as the Carnegies sat around the table eating their frugal supper. Ailie Fargie had been paid back. They were out of debt, and the new world lay before them.

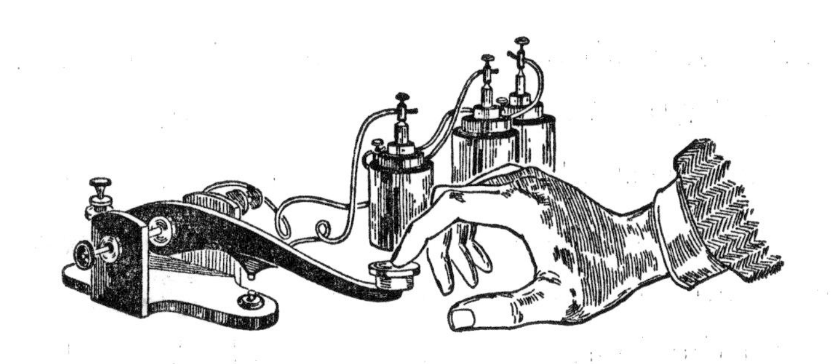

10

THE OFFICE BOY AND THE MORSE CODE

But time slips by. When he began, Andrew thought there was nothing in the world so exciting as being a telegraph boy. But he stayed at this work only about a year.

"If you could come down to the office a little early in the morning, you could sweep it out and have it all in order before the business day starts," Mr. Brooks said to him one day.

That was all Mr. Brooks needed to say. After that Andrew was there every morning at least an hour before the others arrived. He swept the floor, emptied the scrap baskets, filled the inkwells, sharpened the pencils, and set things in order generally for the work of the day. While he was doing all this, the telegraph instrument clicked incessantly, though there was no one there to take care of it. The sound of the clicking annoyed Andrew as he went about his work.

He learned the Morse code before very long. Most boys of the time knew it. Sometimes he put down his broom or his duster and tried sending messages to nearby operators. The messages were halting at first, but the receiver was able to make them out.

One day just after he had unlocked the office door and before he had even hung up his cap and muffler, he heard a message coming over the wire. In his ordinary routine of office boy he should have ignored it, but as he stood just inside the door, listening, he could not bear to go about his work with the message unheeded. He turned the switch which connected him with the sender.

"It's a death message," the operator signaled. "It ought to be delivered at once. Do you think you could take it?"

It would be nearly an hour before the regular operator came to the office. Anyway Andrew knew perfectly well he could do it.

"I'll take it," he clicked.

It was perfectly easy. Andrew took the message with no trouble at all. But after the first flush of enthusiasm, the messenger boy had his doubts. After all, he was merely a messenger boy, with the added responsibility of sweeping out the office. He had no right to interfere with the telegraph instrument. It was pure impulse that had made him do it.

Mr. Brooks came in promptly at nine

o'clock. Andrew looked at him fearfully. Would he be angry? Would he reprimand Andrew? Might he even dismiss him? What would happen to the family then?

But Mr. Brooks was not angry. He was even rather pleased. After that he very often let Andrew take the messages and even put him in charge of the office when he was away.

Pleasant as all this was to a young man's vanity, it had its difficulties, however, as Andrew soon was to find.

The telegraph was a cumbersome, complicated mechanism. A great length of tape was rolled on a wheel in it; and as the thin strip of paper unwound, dots and dashes were printed on it. When the dots had been recorded on the tape, it was given to a copyist who transcribed it on a typewriter.

That copyist was a curmudgeon. He did not like to see a mere boy entrusted with the telegraph machine.

"I won't take it," he said to Andrew one day

when the message had been recorded on the tape.

Andrew looked at the older man and then went back to the machine. He took up a pencil and a piece of paper.

"Give the message again, slowly," he said to the operator.

The operator repeated the message. And Andrew transcribed it—not putting down the dots and dashes, but writing out the words.

"Gee," said the copyist, looking over Andrew's shoulder. He knew of only one other person who could take a message that way. It is the regular practice of telegraphers now.

Not very long after that day, Andrew wrote a letter to his Cousin Dod in Scotland.

"I have got past delivering messages now," he wrote, "and have got to operating. I am to have four dollars a week and a good prospect of soon getting more."

Four dollars a week! It was a wonderful sum. Andrew bought a rocking chair for his mother, who still had very little time to sit in it, to be sure. And the Carnegies decided that they could now move out of the little shed on the alley. Andrew's aunts and Uncle Hogan were moving to Ohio, and the Carnegies could get their house for a reasonable sum.

Andrew now was sixteen and earned twenty-five dollars a month. But even these heights were to be surpassed.

11

EVENINGS ARE FOR READING

Colonel James Anderson, tall, erect and gray-haired, was a much respected citizen of Pittsburgh. For many years he had been active in the business life of his city where he had served on various boards and committees and had taken successful part in various business enterprises. Now at about sixty-five he had decided to retire from active business. But a man of sixty-five is not ready to give up a life of activity. There were a good many years ahead for Colonel Anderson. He decided he would devote these years to reading. He would put himself in touch with the great minds of past ages.

With characteristic energy he set about collecting books, and soon he had a good library of several hundred volumes and had read them all.

Now Colonel Anderson found that buying books and reading them was a rather lonely business. He wanted to share his books with someone else.

In Pittsburgh at that time there was no such thing as a public library. Why, Colonel Anderson wondered, should he not create one? He was particularly interested in young boys. His library would be for them.

Forthwith he let it be known that apprentice boys might come to his house on Saturday evenings to borrow his books. He himself was there to hand them out. Any apprentice boy might take a book; and after a week, if he returned it clean and in good condition, he might borrow another.

Andrew heard about Colonel Anderson's library almost as soon as it started: he was one of the first to come and borrow.

The library seemed to Andrew his crowning satisfaction now. He liked the work in the telegraph office, he could stop often to see a Shakespearean play, and now there were the books. Sometimes Colonel Anderson lent him books about American history; once he lent him Plutarch's *Lives,* and then there were Macaulay's *Essays* and Lamb's *Essays*. Perhaps what he enjoyed even more than these were the technical books. There was one on the manufacture of iron that held him fascinated. Every night at six he went home to his book, and at the end of a week it was finished and he could start another.

But this state of things was too blissful to last. And it was Colonel Anderson himself who spoiled it all. He observed how much the boys seemed to enjoy his books and decided he would make a larger library so that more boys might read. He took a substantial sum of money, went to New York City, and bought nearly two thousand books. Then he asked the municipal government of Allegheny if they would find space for his books. They set aside a large room in a house on Federal Street and employed a librarian to look after the new apprentices' library.

But here the trouble came. The librarian, a conscientious man, took up his post behind the librarian's desk, and one Saturday evening, soon after six o'clock, Andrew came in to borrow a book.

"Could I have a book on metallurgy?" he asked the librarian politely.

"Are you an apprentice? To whom are you apprenticed?"

"I am a telegraph operator."

That was the difficulty. A telegraph operator was not an apprentice to anybody. Yet Andrew wanted to read.

Andrew withdrew from his conversation with the librarian, much troubled. How could he get the books that had made his evenings so full of joy? What could he do now?

Somehow the idea of writing a letter to the newspaper suggested itself. For several evenings he sat beneath the lamp polishing off a communication to the *Despatch*. After a while he felt that it was good enough to send, and he signed it *A Working Boy* and put it in the mailbox.

He did not wait long for a reply. In only two or three days the *Despatch* printed an answer to his letter. It stated plainly and clearly that the new library was intended solely for apprentices.

But Andrew was not satisfied. Why should not working boys, whether they were bound as apprentices or not, be able to read? He wrote again.

And this time his letter was answered very quickly. If *A Working Boy* would call at the librarian's office, the librarian would be glad to talk to him.

So Andrew won his battle and was able to go on with his reading. And the letters which he had written to the *Despatch* were read and praised by all his friends. And Andrew himself thought that as literary compositions they were not bad. Perhaps they were even rather good. The life of a newspaper man was one that had always attracted him. He clipped out his letters from the columns of the *Despatch,* folded them and put them carefully into his breast pocket, and started a round of newspaper offices. But not a single newspaper would hire him. Perhaps he had better stick to telegraphy.

And meantime there were those technical books on the manufacture of iron that he had been reading. He thought he would borrow them and read them again.

12

A CONVERSATION WITH A RAILROAD MAN

"Someday I'll buy you a silk dress, and we'll live in a house with a garden and you can ride around in a carriage."

Andrew's mother smiled at him.

"I like the rocking chair you gave me

better," she said. "Where would I go in a carriage?"

She had worked hard—washing and ironing, cooking and cleaning for the four of them. In her spare time she had bound hundreds of shoes to bring in some extra money for the family. She looked now at Andrew and at young Tom and felt content.

"But I want you to have these things," Andrew protested. "Maybe a servant too."

He was still thinking of the silk dress and the carriage when he went to the telegraph office one day in April, 1853. His monthly pay didn't make them seem very likely—at least for a while to come.

He was very busy that day at the telegraph office. But in the middle of the afternoon there was a lull in his work. He was alone in the office when the door opened and Thomas Scott, the buoyant young superintendent of the Pennsylvania Railroad, entered.

"Another message, Mr. Scott?" Andrew

smiled respectfully though Mr. Scott was only about ten years his senior.

"We seem to have a lot of messages. This one ought to go in a hurry," Mr. Scott answered.

"It will," Andrew said. "I'll have it in your Philadelphia office inside half an hour."

"Fine," Scott replied, and turned to go. But there was something about Andrew that he liked—and he was not in a hurry.

"Sending messages by wire is a great thing for the railroad," he said.

"You send so many I should think it would pay the railroad to have a line of its own," Andrew answered. "I suppose it would cost too much?"

"It isn't only that," Tom Scott said. "The railroad needs new men in it—men with imagination."

He sat down in a low wooden chair close to Andrew's desk, not worrying apparently about the fact that he was an officer of the railroad and Andrew only a telegraph clerk.

"I have so many plans for the railroad," he said.

There was a long pause, while the telegraph instrument rattled.

"The worst things about the road now are those single tracks," he said, "single tracks with trains going both ways on them. Of course the trains run into each other—even with the greatest care in the world. They can't help it. If we could direct the trains by telegraph, we might avoid the accidents."

"That's true," Andrew answered, "and you ought to build some new lines. Oughtn't you to build a new line between Harrisburg and Philadelphia? And maybe one from the East right to the Ohio River? I remember it took us more than three weeks to come out here from New York by canal."

"Of course we ought," Tom Scott retorted.

"We ought to have a line right across the mountains to the West. And there ought to be bridges across the rivers, not just barge ferries—"

So the two talked while the telegraph keys rattled an accompaniment. Now and then Andrew stopped to take a message which he wrote out on a slip and set aside, ready to be delivered by the messenger when he came in. It grew dark before his visitor left, and he lighted the big oil lamp that hung from the ceiling.

As he walked home that night, Andrew seemed to hear the locomotive whistles shrieking through wild valleys and to see the long tracks spreading across the plains, while freights and passenger trains, nicely spaced by telegraph communication, sped back and forth.

Not many weeks later a communication from Thomas Scott came to him. Would he operate the new telegraph which the railroad was installing, and act as Mr. Scott's assistant in the office? It didn't take Andrew long to decide.

"I'm to have thirty-five dollars a month," he told his mother, thinking it a princely sum. Of course he could not buy her the silk dress and the horse and carriage yet—but he had hopes.

The work in the Pennsylvania Railroad office was exciting to Andrew. Mr. Scott had to be away a great deal of the time, and Andrew took on more and more responsibility.

"What do you think my little Scotchman did the other day?" Mr. Scott said to some of his friends. "There was a wreck on the road, and every train on the division was tied up. Andy couldn't get hold of me, so he just sent wires directing every train how to move till the whole business was cleared up and the railroad was running on schedule again. Signed my name to the telegrams, he did."

That episode had turned out well—but Andrew wished he could have signed the telegrams A.C. instead of T.A.S.

Not long after that a freight car got jammed across the track, and the line was blocked again. No one could move the freight car. Again Thomas Scott was away; again Andrew took the reins.

"Burn the car," he telegraphed, and again he signed Scott's name.

It was all right. Burning the freight car was the only quick, feasible thing to do.

In 1859 Mr. Scott became president of the Pennsylvania Railroad.

"Do you think you could manage the Western Division?" he asked Andrew. Andrew was a little hurt that he should even question it. He was twenty-four now, and he thought he could manage anything.

Andrew Carnegie, manager of the Western Division of the Pennsylvania Railroad, no longer thought it proper to live in Rebecca Street. He bought a comfortable house, called Homewood, in the suburbs about ten miles from Pittsburgh. His father died before they moved into it. ("It was too bad, just as we were beginning to be able to make him comfortable," Andrew said later.) But his mother now had not one silk dress but several. She had a flower garden too, for she loved flowers.

She objected a little when Andrew insisted that she must have a servant. She had always taken care of her family herself, and she would have nothing to do if these tasks were taken away from her. But she agreed to the servant finally: perhaps her pride in her son's success compensated for some hours of dullness in her own life. Tom, too, was developing into a competent executive.

And now Andrew, driving to Pittsburgh every morning behind a smart thoroughbred, planned that someday he would be a very rich man—rich enough to own a great library with hundreds and hundreds of volumes.

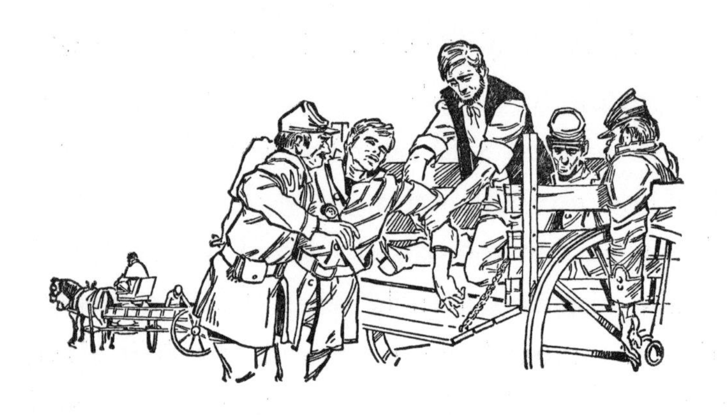

13

TELEGRAPH LINES AND WOUNDED SOLDIERS

"Fort Sumter has been fired on!"

All Pittsburgh was in a frenzy on the morning the news came over the telegraph wires. Andrew Carnegie had taken the train instead of driving to his office that day, and he found the car buzzing with talk.

"Didn't I tell you last night what the Secessionists intended?"

"But they have fired on the flag—they have fired on our flag!"

Army enlistments started that very day, and Andrew Carnegie was among the first to offer himself. The Civil War was under way.

Thomas Scott was put in charge of the Union's communications system. And Carnegie was soon in Washington in a room adjoining Scott's at the War Office. They started to string up an elaborate system of telegraph wires connecting strategic points in the north. This was the first war in American history where telegraph was used in the direction of troops.

Work was barely started before an extreme crisis came. Washington was in danger of being cut off from the Union.

For it was impossible to reach the capital from the north without going through part of Maryland, and Maryland at that time sympathized with the South. In the first month of the war, her people had pulled up the railroad tracks and torn down the telegraph lines and so cut off the capital. How could the war be fought if Lincoln and his cabinet were not in communication with the Northern troops?

Lincoln had already called for 7,500 volunteers, and these had been enlisted quickly. But how to send them to Washington and thence to the front was a puzzle. At the end of April not a single regiment had got through.

"When will they come? When will they come?" The President was pacing back and forth in his office in the White House. If the Confederates should capture Washington, if they should take Lincoln prisoner—what would happen to the Union cause then?

The railroad tracks leading into Washington must be put back if the capital was to be in touch with the Union armies again. Doing that was a vital job—it was the job given to Andrew Carnegie.

He began to work at once, bringing an odd collection of conductors, trainmen and bridge builders from the railroad in Pittsburgh.

When he got to the Susquehanna River with them, they found that the bridge had been destroyed so they took a ferryboat, the *Maryland*. This was a lucky coincidence, for on board the boat were General Benjamin F. Butler and the Eighth Massachusetts Regiment. Many of the men in this regiment were skilled mechanics. They offered to help.

The country through which the railroad passed was mostly woodland, with here and there a little town. The tracks and sleepers had been torn up, and in some places they had been hidden in the woods. But the men went scouring among the trees to find them, and before long three miles of track were laid again.

Now the march to Washington began. The men walked, their knapsacks on their backs. The train carried cannon, munitions, food supplies and other gear. Southern sympathizers sniped at them from time to time, but they got through.

Carnegie rode in the cab of the locomotive and watched for telegraph lines that had been tampered with.

"There's a line down," he called to the engineer in one place. The train came to a stop, and Carnegie jumped down. The line had been staked to the ground, and he pulled out the stakes so that it could be raised. He did not notice that the wires had been pulled to one side before staking. When he released them, they flew up, cutting a deep gash in his face. He mopped up the blood with his handkerchief, but it continued to flow down over his collar and shirt. He was bleeding still when he entered Washington and reported at the War Office.

People in the North breathed easier now, for the Northern troops were pouring to the front.

Washington, the capital, was safe. Lincoln could carry on the war.

Carnegie worked frantically in the War Office after that. His telegraph operators kept the capital in touch with the various Northern armies at the front. Lincoln himself haunted the telegraph office for news—he would not wait for messages to be brought to him.

But Carnegie was not to spend all his time in the War Office. In July there was a great clamor among the Northerners to go ahead and destroy the Confederacy. General Irvin McDowell had a big body of troops in Washington and, though they were not yet very well trained or disciplined, Lincoln and General Scott finally heeded the continuous cries of "On to Richmond." Thirty-five miles from Washington, near a little stream called Bull Run, McDowell met the Confederate forces under General Beauregard, and the fighting began.

Carnegie had gone to Bull Run in advance

of the troops to set up the communications. He had taken with him the finest set of telegraph operators he could find. And they arranged their instruments at Burke's Station, a little village about five miles from the front.

At first things went well. All through the morning Carnegie could hear the sound of the cannon. The messages he sent back to Washington were filled with triumph. In the afternoon, however, there was a change. More Confederate troops, hosts of them, had been brought up. The tide was beginning to turn.

By mid-afternoon it was a rout. McDowell's men were running past his station, yelling as they ran. The wounded and dying were being dragged back from the fighting area.

Carnegie left his office and began to help load the stretchers into ambulances. He had never seen men in that condition before—the sight of them made him feel sick and faint. But he kept on handing up stretcher after stretcher. When all the ambulances had been filled, they put the wounded into farm wagons and any other conveyances that could be found.

Before night Burke's Station was quiet. The First Battle of Bull Run was over—every soldier of the Northern Army had either retreated or was dead. Only then did Carnegie and his staff of telegraphers leave. He was proud to think that not a single member of the telegraph staff had panicked; not a single one of them had joined in the rout. Every telegrapher had stayed at his post as long as there were any messages to send or receive.

Carnegie remained in charge of the telegraph communication until the war was over. Gradually he organized a staff of 1,500 men. And in many places they sent down observations by telegraph from balloons floating high over the enemy lines. They sent the news of Gettysburg, and of Lee's surrender at Appomattox, and later clicked out the news of Lincoln's death.

Long after the war was over, Andrew Carnegie remembered those days—remembered how his men had stuck to their posts, receiving and sending the rattling messages. And he remembered the frightened men running past at Bull Run and the crushed and broken bodies he had lifted into the wagons. He was sure the war had been necessary and that the Union cause was right. But from that time on he hated war. Later he was to establish the Carnegie Endowment for International Peace—his contribution to the prevention of war.

14

IRON BRIDGES

One day, after the war was over (it was April, 1865), Andrew stopped at the workshop of one of the railroad employees named Piper—"Old Pipe" everybody called him. The two men had known each other nearly ten years and were good friends though they were so different. Andrew was only about thirty, short, of delicate build, and inclined to be quiet. Old Pipe, on the other hand, was a great, heavy-boned mechanic, generally sweaty from the forge.

That day in April the two men began to talk about horses, as they usually did. Carnegie had just bought a new carriage horse.

"A beauty," he told Old Pipe. "A thoroughbred in every line. You must see her."

But Old Pipe could match his friend's stories. Since last Carnegie had seen him, he had tamed a Kentucky colt—such a colt! Such strength and beauty—such speed! He would train her for the track. Carnegie would see!

After they had talked awhile, Carnegie asked what Old Pipe was doing for the railroad now that the war was over.

"The usual thing," Old Pipe said. "Whenever a train breaks through one of those old wooden bridges, they send for me to patch up the bridge again. Whenever the sparks from the engine set a bridge afire, they send for me to build another."

"Keep you pretty busy?" Carnegie asked.

Old Pipe did not answer. Instead he took a leather tobacco pouch from his pocket, filled his briar, stuffing the tobacco down carefully, and set it alight with a great, flaming match which he scratched on his shoe. Then he rose and walked toward a door at the back of the workshop.

"Come in here," he said.

Carnegie followed Old Pipe into the inner room. There Old Pipe pulled aside a piece of dirty canvas that covered an object on the floor. It was a beautifully constructed little bridge made entirely of iron.

"My iron bridges won't be the first ones ever made, but they'll be the best ones. Look at that span. Isn't she graceful? And strong?"

"It might be a horse he was describing," Carnegie thought, but he did not interrupt.

"There ought to be bridges like this one—

hundreds and thousands of them. Now that the war is over and the soldiers are coming back, what will they do? Go west, of course. They'll stake out claims on the plains and start planting hundreds of thousands of acres. And how will the railroads get across all the rivers that lie between here and the West? On little rickety wooden bridges?

Piper laughed scornfully at the idea. Then he went on.

"I've got a patent on this iron bridge. We've started a company with J. H. Linville to build them. Piper and Linville we call it. We haven't got much capital, of course. Not much chance to talk to the railroad executives, but our bridges are beauties. . . ."

"They certainly are if they're like that one," Carnegie said, examining the model carefully.

Now Carnegie was no engineer and no mechanic, and he knew hardly anything about bridges. But already, at the age of thirty, he

Carnegie Corporation of New York

Andrew Carnegie was born in this tiny weaver's cottage in Dunfermline, Scotland.

Culver Service

The good ship *Wiscasset* brought the Carnegie family to America in 1848. It docked in New York, probably at a pier like this.

Bettmann Archive

In 1850, when this drawing of New York was made, no one had heard of skyscrapers. No one suspected that someday Carnegie steel would help raise tall buildings.

Culver Service

This picture of Andrew Carnegie was made in 1863 when he was 28. By the time he was 33, he was earning more than $50,000 a year.

Brown Brothers

Soon Carnegie had enough money to live in this splendid mansion in New York City.

Carnegie Corporation of New York

Carnegie wanted to escape the hot American summers. So he built Skibo Castle in Scotland, where the climate is cooler. Here he spent many happy hours in his later years swimming, fishing and playing golf.

Brown Brothers

Carnegie made a tour of Scotland in 1881. On this trip, his mother (front of coach) surprised everyone by dancing a Highland fling.

Culver Service

Here you see Mr. and Mrs. Andrew Carnegie out for a drive.

Carnegie Corporation of New York

Andrew Carnegie pauses during a walk at Skibo Castle. With him is his favorite dog, Lassie.

Culver Service

The Lucy Furnaces in Pittsburgh, Pennsylvania, were among the first steel plants operated by Carnegie Brothers and Company.

Culver Service

This is a scene at an early blast furnace. Much of the work was done by hand, and the men were unprotected.

Brown Brothers

Today steel workers wear heavy clothes, gloves and masks. They have learned to protect themselves from heat, glare and shooting sparks.

U.S. Steel

This white-hot ingot is being taken from the soaking pits. It is now soft enough to be rolled into great sheets of steel.

U.S. Steel

The ingot passes back and forth between the rolls. Soon it reaches the proper thinness.

U.S. Steel

Finally the ingot is cold-rolled into big coils, such as you see in this picture. This steel was rolled at the rate of 80 miles per hour.

Brown Brothers

Carnegie gave great sums of money for scientific research. This is the Mount Wilson Observatory in Pasadena, California, one of his most important projects.

Carnegie Library

The Carnegie Library in Pittsburgh, Pennsylvania, is one of thousands of public library buildings Carnegie gave away.

U.S. S

Andrew Carnegie, the poor weaver's son, became the first great leader in the Age of Steel.

had accumulated some capital. Sometime before, he had borrowed money to buy shares in the Adams Express Company. With the money he had made from this investment he had bought stock in a sleeping car company. So it had happened that when Drake struck oil in Titusville, Pennsylvania, he had been able to invest in oil. And at the age of thirty he had accumulated what amounted to a fortune.

Now here was Old Pipe with his model of an iron bridge. And it was certain that the railroads must extend their lines. The great plains of the West, the present homes of buffalo and wandering Indian tribes, the mountain slopes, the fertile valleys, the far coasts of the Pacific—surely people would be settling in all these places. A million men who had been under arms in the Civil War would, as Old Pipe had said, be going back to civilian life. And they would not stay crowded in the eastern cities—not with the wealth of a continent to develop. They would want to travel fast—no slow oxcarts now, no river steamers, or canals. They would go fast, by railroad.

Carnegie thought about it as he drove back to Homewood that night. His mother and Tom found him unusually quiet as they sat eating dinner, and he went to bed almost immediately after.

Lying there in the dark, with the curtains flapping in the spring breeze, Andrew Carnegie thought of the rattle of railroad wheels on their tracks, of the screech of locomotive whistles across lonely fields. The railroads, he understood now, must be the great instruments of America's destiny, and he would help to build them. He would not invest directly in railroad stock, as Gould and Vanderbilt were doing. He would build the bridges and the rails and control the iron that the railroads were made of.

Soon after that he went again to see Old Pipe. Would he and Linville consider taking him into partnership in the bridge company? He would supply a substantial amount of capital, and there would be opportunity to work on a larger scale.

So the Keystone Bridge Company was started. And not long after that the Union Iron Mills were formed to help supply the needed iron, and after that a mill to make iron rails, and then the Pittsburgh Locomotive Works.

In those early days after the Civil War, the future of America and of Andrew Carnegie seemed somehow bound together with the hard bright metal. But that was, of course, before Andrew Carnegie had even heard of steel.

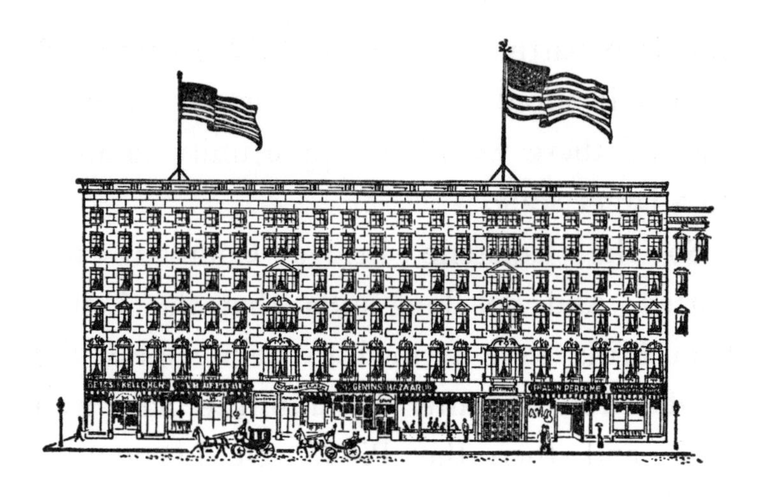

15

A GREAT CITY AND A GOOD RESOLUTION

Carnegie's mother accustomed herself to her son's prosperity. For Andrew had interests in many companies now and was spoken of as a rising young capitalist. Tom, too, was proving an important executive. The mother was proud of them both—proud and a little sad when she thought of her husband and of the loom that was quiet now.

Now she had servants and hardly lifted her finger for housework. Long ago she had put away her shoe-binding needles, for she had no need of them. With a smile she sometimes remembered how Andrew had given her a silk dress. Now she had all the silk dresses she wanted. And the rocking chair Andrew had given her—she still kept the rocking chair, though it did not fit in very well with its rich surroundings.

She had more time for mail now. Sometimes, when a letter came from Scotland, she put it in her sewing basket; and took it out from time to time so that she might reread it, remembering again, as she did so, the click of the looms along the street at Dunfermline and the pinks that she had grown in the little space behind the cottage there.

Then one day Andrew came home and upset her world again. Tom, as she knew, was to be married in the autumn. Why should they not give Homewood to Tom and his bride?

"Then you and I could go live in New York," Andrew told her. "New York is the center for all sorts of businesses now. All the great industries have offices in New York."

Not long after that Andrew Carnegie and his mother traveled to New York on the Pennsylvania Railroad. They drove in a carriage to the St. Nicholas Hotel at Broadway and Spring Street, a few blocks north of the old City Hall.

Mrs. Carnegie walked with her son up the wide marble steps and through the fluted Corinthian columns at the hotel's entrance, and saw that the place he had brought her to live was a place of grandeur. She walked through stately corridors on deep-piled carpet, and up another elegant stairway of Carrara marble. A dozen chandeliers hung overhead with pendent, iridescent crystals. All the walls were covered with tapestries and gleaming mirrors. Gentlemen in stovepipe hats and ladies in bustled dresses, cut in the latest style, moved back and forth with grace and assurance. And in the distance a stringed orchestra played some melody that Andrew's mother did not know—as if for a ball, she thought.

It was not long before they were settled in their comfortable suite, a fire in the grate, a maid bringing them their supper. "The tea's not strong enough," Andrew's mother said as she sat in a tufted chair upholstered in some rich brocade, looking down on the life of Broadway. Crowds of people were walking up and down—some of them handsomely dressed like the people in the hotel, but the greater number were working people, foreign born, she thought. Wagons went by, loaded with kegs of beer, sacks of grain, cabbages and other vegetables, crowded against each other, the horses rearing and plunging and the drivers shouting.

Sometimes an omnibus went careening by, and Mrs. Carnegie caught a glimpse of the passengers inside.

Watching all this, her mind went back to that day, not long ago it seemed to her, when she and her husband had first come to New York. Andrew and Tom had both been little fellows then. She remembered the sailor who gave Andrew the drink of sarsaparilla and smiled as she thought of them. It grew dark as she sat there, remembering. A boy came running up the street with a long taper to light the lamps in the lampposts, but the going and coming in the street below her was as lively as it had been in the daytime.

Andrew Carnegie did not pause to look at the moving life of Broadway, nor did he smile over memories of their past. When he and his mother had finished their supper, he withdrew to the comfortable room he had reserved for himself, sat down at a table and drew a sheaf of papers out of his leather bag. Soon it was too dark to see, and he lighted the green-shaded oil lamp and sat down again for an evening of work.

He wanted to make a list of his investments—Pennsylvania Railroad, Keystone Bridge Company, Union Iron Mills and half a dozen others. He wrote the list carefully in his small, neat hand, dipping his pen into the ornate glass inkwell which the hotel provided. When he had completed the list, he wrote opposite the name of each company what it had paid him in the preceding year. Then he added the column, looked at the total, and added it again. The figure he had put at the bottom of the column was $56,110.

Andrew Carnegie was only thirty-three, and he had an income of over $50,000 a year! It was probable that those same investments would pay him more next year. He sat staring at the column. Then he took a fresh sheet of paper, dipped his pen in the ink again and began to write a memorandum to himself:

St. Nicholas Hotel,
New York
December, 1868

Thirty-three and an income of $50,000 per annum! By this time two years I can arrange all my business as to secure at least $50,000 per annum. Beyond this never earn—make no effort to increase my fortune, but spend the surplus for benevolent purposes. Cast aside business forever, except for others.

Settle in Oxford and get a thorough education, making the acquaintance of literary men—this will take three years' active work—pay special attention to speaking in public. Settle then in London and purchase a controlling interest in some newspaper or live review and give the general management of it attention, taking a part in public matters, especially those connected with education and improvement of the poorer classes.

Man must have an idol—the amassing of wealth is one of the worst species of idolatry—no idol more debasing than the worship of money. Whatever I engage in I must push inordinately; therefore I should be careful to choose that life which will be the most elevating in character. To continue much longer overwhelmed by business cares and with most of my thought wholly upon the way to make more money in the shortest time, must degrade me beyond hope of permanent recovery. I will resign business at thirty-five, but during the ensuing two years I wish to spend the afternoons in receiving instruction and in reading systematically.

So Andrew Carnegie wrote at the age of thirty-three.

16

"WE MUST MAKE STEEL RAILS!"

"We must make steel rails!"

Andrew Carnegie burst into the office of Carnegie, Kloman and Company, the Pittsburgh manufacturing company which he and his partners now owned.

"The reign of iron is over. Steel is King!"

Tom Carnegie and Kloman looked up in surprise. They had thought Carnegie was in Scotland, where he had gone every year saying that the American climate was impossible in summer. (He had had heat prostration several years before.) But he was not in Scotland now. He was standing in the middle of the office, his blue eyes fairly burning with excitement.

"I didn't even stop to go to the hotel. I came right up to tell you. I saw Henry Bessemer in London."

The partners looked at Carnegie in astonishment. It was not like him to go off half-cocked.

"We must make steel rails," he was saying again. "The wrought iron ones we have been making wear out so much faster than steel would. Why, they have to be replaced every few months and, on some of the sharp curves, even every six weeks. Steel rails will last for years. I figured it all out on the steamer coming over."

Kloman spoke at last. "Steel's all right for knives," he said. "And for needles and small parts of machines. It takes two weeks to make a few hundred pounds of steel by the crucible method. Crucible steel would be too hard for rails. And it would cost a fortune."

"Ah," said Carnegie, "that's just it. It wouldn't cost a fortune." He was so excited that he had not stopped to sit down. He was striding back and forth across the shop.

"Are you daft?" Kloman asked. "For more than a year you couldn't be talked to about the Bessemer process. I heard you practically throw a man out of your office who suggested it to you."

"Aye, that was before I visited Henry Bessemer. He took me to his workshop at Baxter House and gave me a demonstration of his converter which was a big pear-shaped vessel. It was a wonderful sight, a wonderful sight! It sounded like a hundred roaring bulls, and smoke and flames came out of it like an artificial volcano. After about fifteen minutes the flames died down—he'd burned out all the impurities and the carbon in the pig iron as well. Then he added a compound called spiegeleisen, which put back just enough carbon to change the iron into steel. Bessemer is certainly a great inventor: he invented machinery for tipping over the converter to pour out the steel. A man can do it at a safe distance from the converter. With my own eyes, I saw Bessemer pour out five tons of good steel. Did you hear what I said, *five tons.*"

The others could not help but be impressed.

"Yes," said Kloman, "I've heard it's a wonderful thing to see. A friend of mine saw William Kelly do the same thing at his works in Kentucky. He began experimenting with the process six or seven years before Bessemer."

Kloman paused, pulling a pad toward him, and picking up a pencil. "It was like this," he said, drawing a hasty sketch. The others bent down close to watch.

"That's it!" said Carnegie. "But it doesn't

matter who started it. We should get in with this thing at the beginning. Bessemer rails are going to replace these wrought iron rails which are good for only a few months. Steel rails will last for years and years."

Carnegie's eyes gleamed as if seeing a vision. "Steel's going to do more than that," he said. "It's going to be used in bridges, buildings, machinery—nearly everywhere that we use iron today."

"That may be, Andy," said Kloman, "but we're doing very well now making axles, bridge materials and our other iron products. Why should we tempt fortune?"

But Carnegie was now a man with one overpowering purpose—to manufacture Bessemer steel and roll it into rails.

"Very well, boys," he said, "if you won't go along with me, I'll find other partners who will. . . . New capital, new partners, a new plant."

17

THE BUILDING OF A STEEL PLANT

If Carnegie's partners in the iron business would not help him to make steel, he knew there were others who would. He was soon busy calling on his friends, telling of the great opportunities that steel offered.

"New railroad lines are stretching everywhere across the continent," he told them. "There will be orders for hundreds of miles of rails. Those rails, if they are made of iron, will wear out in a few weeks with the weight of the trains passing over them. But if they're made of steel—"

He soon found enough bold men to put their money into the new venture. Carnegie himself had a clear $250,000 that he could invest.

After much discussion, Carnegie and his partners decided to build the Edgar Thomson Works, not in Pittsburgh, but in Braddock, about twelve miles away, at the place where the Monongahela River joins the Ohio. This plant was made expressly for producing Bessemer steel rails and had a number of converters and a rail mill. The site was a historic one, for here General Braddock had met his bloody defeat in 1755 in the French and Indian War. Farmers in the locality were constantly picking up bullets, belt buckles and buttons of military uniforms that were washed up to the surface of the earth. But the eyes of Carnegie and his partners were not on the past: they chose the site because the Pennsylvania and the B & O railroads met there, and it was an important point for shipping on the Ohio River.

The walls of the new plant began to rise in the spring of 1873. That spring prices and wages were higher than they had ever been; crops from the western farms were supplying all America's needs and being sent to Europe. In the cities, theaters, hotels and shops were booming—everybody seemed to have plenty of money to spend. In the engineers' offices more and more plans were being drawn up for the railroads to which Carnegie would sell his steel rails.

But prosperity is a fickle thing. In the autumn of that very year, 1873, prosperity was changed to depression. People had spent too much, too carelessly. They had bought what they could not afford to pay for. They had borrowed money they could not afford to repay.

By 1874 the banks began to put up their shutters: people had withdrawn their money. Jay Cooke and Company of Philadelphia, the biggest and soundest bank in the country, had to close. Not long after that the New York Stock Exchange closed. And now people were really frightened. New enterprises were abandoned. Old established businesses failed. Factories went out of business because no one could afford to buy their products. Blast furnaces around Pittsburgh were cold. Hungry, unemployed men roamed the streets.

Everywhere men's credit was questioned. Credit is the confidence placed in a business that it will be able to meet its operating expenses, to pay its indebtedness. No business can operate successfully without credit. And very few businesses at that time could meet the test.

With so many businesses going down because of lack of credit, it was natural enough that

Andrew Carnegie should be questioned. The steel plant was new; in fact it was just coming into existence. None of the important Pittsburgh businessmen knew much about it, or about Andrew Carnegie, for that matter. They thought he was a reckless adventurer. What made him think that he and his partners could afford to go on building a steel mill when the businesses around them were falling to ruin? If he was to be given any credit in the city of Pittsburgh, he must answer that question.

"I have no objection to answering questions," Andrew Carnegie said.

The questions were asked, and the answers given in the directors' room of the Pittsburgh Exchange Bank.

The atmosphere in the room was tense that morning in the spring of 1874. The directors of the Exchange Bank were very portly, dignified and important men, and they were determined to put Carnegie in his place. Fair-haired, very short and slight in build, Carnegie sat quietly and listened to their questions.

From whom had he borrowed the money he was spending on the steel mill, they asked him. What bank had signed the notes? They would certainly not give him credit if it was found that he was already in debt.

Carnegie listened until they had finished. Then to everyone's surprise he pushed back his chair, paused for a moment and, when all eyes were upon him, began to make a speech. All his life since he was a small boy at Uncle Lauder's grocery store he had enjoyed making speeches. He made a good one now.

He had not borrowed money from any bank for the steel plant, he announced. Every dollar that he had and every piece of property he owned, he owned in full. He regarded speculation—the buying of shares with borrowed money—a wicked thing. Any man who engaged in business enterprises on the chance of making great gains was a rascal, he said.

The speech was a long one. The bankers listened to it with shocked surprise. They had regarded Carnegie as one of Pittsburgh's weakest and poorest businessmen. Now here the little fellow stood, scolding them, lecturing them on business principles. Of course, if he needed credit to carry on routine business practice, it would certainly be possible to forward it, they said at last.

So through those sad years of 1874 and 1875, with business failures all around it, the big steel mill on the Braddock battlefield continued to rise.

"There are a great many advantages in building in time of depression," Carnegie told his associates. "It's easy to get labor when half the world is out of work. And prices of all the materials you need are way down—"

That was to be another principle that was to

contribute to the little man's success. "Always expand your business in times of depression when other people probably cannot afford to do it—"

There was shrewdness in Andrew Carnegie, even in the beginning of his great career. He was thirty-seven years old when he began to manufacture steel.

18

CAPTAIN BILL JONES, STEEL MAKER

Soon the towers of the big steel mills were rising on the Monongahela River. One after another the egg-shaped converters took form. Materials for steel making were ready as soon as the machinery was in place. Shipments of iron ore were brought across the Great Lakes in large ore vessels and were received at Conneaut, a port on Lake Erie. From there the ore was carried on a railroad owned by Carnegie to the Pittsburgh area. Coke, which was now rapidly replacing charcoal in the blast furnaces, was supplied by the H. C. Frick Company. This company, which was later to be a part of the Carnegie Company, made its coke from soft coal, most of which was taken from the famous Connellsville seam near Pittsburgh. Limestone for the blast furnaces was plentiful in Pennsylvania. Enormous quantities of the richest ore in the world were brought down the Great Lakes to be made into steel. The coke and limestone that would burn the impurities from that ore were almost inexhaustible.

The labor that could be employed in the new steel mill seemed almost inexhaustible too. Peasants from Europe were landing in America by the thousand. They came from Russia and Poland, from Greece, Rumania and Italy. A few agents in New York were ready to contract for the laborers, sending them up the Hudson by river steamer and across country by the Erie Canal as Carnegie himself had once come.

"It's easy to get labor," Carnegie said to Alexander Holley, the engineer who had been in charge of building the new plant. "Laborers won't be hard to find. But where can we find a man to direct them? Success for this plant will depend on a good superintendent."

"I think I know the man," Alexander Holley said.

So it was that Captain Bill Jones was brought to see Carnegie at Braddock.

Bill Jones was a lumbering, blue-eyed man who weighed two hundred pounds, a contrast indeed to Carnegie, who never weighed more than a hundred and thirty. The grime and grit of an iron foundry had lately been washed from Bill Jones' red-cheeked face.

"Now, what's your experience?" Carnegie asked, looking up at the giant who towered across his desk.

"Worked in an iron foundry since I was ten years old," Jones said.

That was all he seemed to be able to tell, for he was shy in matters that concerned himself.

It took Carnegie a long time to find out the rest. Not until they had become close friends, and not until the new plant was turning out better steel at a faster rate than any other steel mill; not until Captain Bill Jones had built up a reputation as the greatest steel maker in America—not until all that had come to pass, did Andrew Carnegie come to know his superintendent's whole story.

Bill Jones was born in a workman's shack in the smoke and soot of Hazleton, Pennsylvania. His father, a Welsh immigrant, worked in the iron foundry at Hazleton through the week and preached in the Baptist Church on Sundays.

"You're big and strong now—big enough to start to work," his father had said when the boy was ten years old. Bill Jones was proud to be earning money.

The Civil War put a stop to the job in the iron foundry. Bill volunteered and went south with the first Union troops. And now he married a Southern girl, saw hot fighting at Fredericksburg and Chancellorsville. When the war was over, he came north again, expecting to go on with his work in the iron mills.

It's hard for a man who has been to war to settle down again. Bill Jones began to drift. He had a good job at Cambria Iron Works but showed so little interest in it that the superintendent laid him off. After that he came to see Carnegie at Braddock.

Carnegie hired him as a common workman at two dollars a day at first. It was not long before Jones showed what he could do and was put in charge of the plant.

The men liked Bill Jones and worked hard

for him. He had not been at the mill long when he succeeded in making improvements in the converters. Patents for them brought rich dividends to the Carnegie Steel Company, and they increased the output of the mill enormously.

Bill Jones used to nail a green sapling to the shed that produced most steel in a given period, and the men were soon vying with each other in good-natured rivalry. Sometimes, when an especially good record was made, Bill Jones blew the factory whistle and took them all to a baseball game. He thought the hours were too long anyway.

So the steel came pouring from the converters, and soon Carnegie's mills, of which the Edgar Thomson Works at Braddock was only one, outstripped all competitors in output. There was an almost endless market—new railroads were building, new factories setting up machinery, there was need for steel tractors and farm machinery. The shareholders of Carnegie's company met and were astonished at the profits they were making.

"It's due to Bill Jones in large part," Carnegie told them generously. "There's something about that man that makes the laborers want to work."

To Bill Jones himself he said: "The success of the Braddock plant is due to you in large measure. I think you ought to be a partner in the firm. We'll set aside some shares for you. There's no sense in your working for ordinary wages."

To his surprise Bill Jones showed no pleasure at his suggestion.

"Let me think it over till tomorrow," was all that he would say.

Next day the big superintendent appeared early at Carnegie's office.

"About being a partner," he said. "I'd rather go on having wages."

"But you'd make lots more," Carnegie protested. "The partners of this company are going to be very rich men."

"I know," Bill Jones answered. "But it wouldn't be the same. The men would think I was putting on airs—I'd rather work for wages."

There was silence as the little man and the big man looked at each other.

"We'd like to recognize you somehow," Carnegie said.

It was Big Bill Jones who thought of the solution.

"Why don't you give me a whale of a big salary?" he asked.

"A salary as big as the President of the United States gets?" Carnegie proposed.

"That would be all right," Big Bill Jones answered.

So it was done. The salary that Big Bill Jones received henceforth was exactly the salary that the President of the United States received.

"It's too much," one of the partners objected. "It isn't right to pay a common working-man a salary like that."

But Carnegie only smiled.

"Where could we get another man like Bill Jones?" he said.

So more and more converters roared and glowed and poured out their molten steel, and the soot hung in thicker and thicker clouds over the shacks that clung to the Pittsburgh hillsides.

One day in 1889 news came to the mill that a dam had broken at nearby Johnstown. The river had overflowed its banks; hundreds of houses had been swept away; thousands of people were stranded, homeless. The flood was one of the greatest disasters the United States had ever experienced.

Bill Jones heard of the disaster in the middle of a working day, and five minutes later the factory whistles were shrieking.

"The mill is shut down," he announced.

"Are there any men who will volunteer to help the people of Johnstown?"

Hundreds of the steel workers crowded the train that pulled out of Pittsburgh for Johnstown not long after. They went to work in the flooded city, rescuing men and women who had been marooned, pulling furniture out of flooded houses, trying to save livestock. Cap'n Bill Jones seemed to be everywhere among them, directing, encouraging, joking.

It was that same year, 1889, in the month of September, that disaster came also to the steel mill. Something was wrong with one of the blast furnaces. It seemed to be clogged, and the molten iron would not pour from it properly. The men sent for Captain Jones to see about it.

Just as he approached it, the blast furnace set up a terrific roar so loud that it could be heard in the city of Pittsburgh seven miles away. Then it burst, and six workmen who stood near it were killed immediately. Bill Jones was knocked down by the shock of the explosion, his skill fractured and his body covered with multiple burns. He died a few days later in the hospital to which the workmen had carried him.

"Where can we find another Bill Jones?" Andrew Carnegie had asked. He knew now that there was no other Bill Jones to be found.

But the work of the steel mill must go on, and Charles M. Schwab was put in control.

The company continued to prosper, but Captain Bill Jones was a legend among the steel workers now; the things he said, the things he did, were told again and again.

"I worked for Bill Jones," the workers used to say to each other. It was a boast, a gauge of superiority to newcomers.

And in the new house that Andrew Carnegie built on Ninety-first Street in New York City he hung a portrait of Bill Jones in his bedroom—big, strong, with clear blue eyes and face glowing as if from the light of molten iron. It was the only picture that Carnegie kept in his room, a reminder to him of the man he believed to be the greatest steel maker in America.

19

ANDREW'S MOTHER DANCES A HIGHLAND FLING

The red and black coach with its four bay horses went rolling through the English country, the driver and the footman in livery of blue and silver. In the little towns the coach passed through, people ran out of their houses to wave, and the sound of the horn lingered even after the coach itself had disappeared in a cloud of dust. It was the spring of 1881. Andrew Carnegie was taking a coaching trip.

By that time Andrew Carnegie was undisputed leader of the American steel industry. And in that same year the output of American steel surpassed that of England. But Andrew Carnegie, though he was proud of these facts, believed that life should not be completely absorbed in business. He was off on a coaching trip.

Ten friends had been invited to go on the trip with Carnegie and his mother. They were to travel eight hundred miles from Brighton in the south of England, northward into Scotland. The trip was to take them about six weeks.

They left Brighton about the first of April, Andrew and his mother sitting up on the front bench of the coach and the guests behind them. Mrs. Carnegie wore a plain, black silk dress and a black bonnet. Her hands rested quietly in her lap. Some of the young ladies of the party might have enjoyed sharing the front seat with the host, but Mrs. Carnegie never gave up her place. She knew well enough that her son was a desirable bachelor.

Every day at about noon, the coach stopped at some pleasant meadow or on the bank of a little stream. Then tablecloths were spread out on the grass, hampers were opened and the party sat down to a jolly repast. Afterward the travelers rested or wandered through the fields picking wild flowers. Once Carnegie's mother pulled off her shoes and stockings and went wading in a stream. And once she kilted up her petticoats and danced the Highland fling on the grass.

"She was just a wee lassie again," Carnegie wrote later in his *Autobiography*. "And to be a wee lassie at seventy-one is a triumph indeed; but as mother says, that is nothing. She intends to be as daft for many years to come, for grandfather was far older when he alarmed the auld wives of the village on Hallowe'en night, sticking his false face through the windows. . . . I hope to be a daft callant at seventy-one—as daft as we all were that day. Indeed we were all daft enough while coaching, but mother really ought to have been restrained a little. She went beyond all bounds!"

They came to Windsor on the nineteenth of June, and it was Mrs. Carnegie's seventy-first birthday. So Mr. Beck, a member of the party, presented her with a silver cup that was ornamented with birds and flowers, and engraved with the words:

"Presented to Mrs. Margaret Carnegie at Windsor, by the members of the coaching party, upon her seventy-first birthday."

When they presented the cup to her, Mrs. Carnegie, greatly surprised, rose and made a speech which Andrew Carnegie proudly recorded later in his journal:

"I can only wish that you may all have as good health, as complete command of your faculties, and enjoy flowers and birds and all things of nature as much as I do at seventy-one."

So with gaiety that never failed, the coaching party traveled up through the English country. The English gardens were bright with flowers that spring, the meadows lush and green.

Now and again they stopped to visit some ancient church or cathedral. They saw the spires of Oxford and stopped at the thatched cottage where Anne Hathaway had lived and came at last to the Scottish border. There was a stop at the cottage of Robert Burns, and not long afterward the coach was rolling into the village of Dunfermline.

Uncle Lauder joined them outside the village. He was a little older but in no other way different from the beloved Uncle Lauder Andy had hated to leave.

People used to speak of Dunfermline as an "old gray town," but that did not describe it the day Carnegie and his mother came back to it in their coach. Flags were flying, banners waving. Townspeople crowded the streets in their gayest clothes.

At the entrance to the city a triumphal arch had been put up. Here the mayor, the members of the town council, and the magistrates, all dressed in full regalia, were waiting to receive them. The welcoming speech was made, not by one of these dignitaries, but by a workingman, a weaver such as Andrew's father had been.

There was a grand parade to welcome Andrew Carnegie back to the village where he was born. First came the Odd Fellows in full uniform, then the foresters in Lincoln green. Behind them were the gardeners—an important group of men in Scotland. And then a long procession of men and women organized according to their trades. There were bleachers, foundrymen, weavers, dyers, bakers, masons and carpenters. Women and girls from the linen mills marched along, dressed in white and carrying American and British flags. Carnegie's coach, the horses prancing, fell in behind the others, while bands blared and people waved and shouted.

In this fashion they passed through the streets of Dunfermline till they came to the little gray weaver's cottage where Carnegie had been born. There the coach stopped while its occupants looked at the little house in silence.

"I wanted them to see it," Carnegie said afterward. "I wanted my American friends to see the house where I was born."

Several years earlier Carnegie had presented the village of Dunfermline with a public bath. It had been his first philanthropy—the first gift given with the little surplus he had accumulated up to that time. Today he had another gift for the village of his birth. He thought it was a much more precious gift—a public library.

The Dunfermline Library, the first of several thousand libraries which Carnegie was to establish, was given in his mother's name. She officiated in the laying of the cornerstone that day. Long afterward the villagers remembered the occasion. They remembered how she had stood there, an erect and sturdy figure in her black silk dress, her black bonnet set on her smoothly brushed white hair. A silver trowel had been provided for spreading the mortar, and they remembered how carefully she spread it out, as if she had been icing a cake. Then, after she had laid the stone to her satisfaction, she turned and faced them with great dignity, saying in a firm voice:

"I pronounce this memorial stone duly and properly laid, and may God bless the undertaking."

20

"THIS YOUNG MAN, FRICK"

Back in America when the coaching trip was over, Bessemer converters roared and glowed, the molten steel came pouring from them, and the growing markets were supplied. Andrew Carnegie watched the great production with mounting enthusiasm. The United States was expanding. It needed new railroad tracks, new bridges, new farm machinery, new boiler plate, new hulls for ships, new gas pipes. More and more of these were made of steel instead of iron, and most of the steel was made in Pittsburgh.

But fascinated as he was with his blast furnaces and converters, Andrew Carnegie did not spend all his time at the steel mills. Indeed, even when he was in America he spent scarcely half his time there. He believed in employing competent men to do his work. He himself liked to relax and enjoy the good things of life.

In 1880 he bought a summer place at Cresson in the Pennsylvania mountains. There his mother and his brother Tom, with his wife and children, spent the summer months with him, and there his friends visited him.

One day a group of his guests, who happened also to be business associates, joined Carnegie in a long walk through the woods. Their path led along a rushing mountain stream edged on both sides with tall flowering rhododendrons. Carnegie and his guests talked of many things as they tramped single file along the path, Carnegie leading. Then suddenly he turned with a new thought—it was not connected in any way with the talk that had gone before.

"We must attach this young man Frick to our concern," he said. "He has great ability and great energy. Moreover he has the coke, and we need it."

Now coke is what remains when bituminous coal is burned in sealed ovens, driving off the volatile matter and leaving behind a gray residue which is almost pure carbon. It was made from vast fields of soft coal that lay beneath the surface of the earth in Pennsylvania, Virginia, West Virginia and Kentucky. And young Frick owned more of these fields than anyone else.

Henry Clay Frick, the possessor of such vast quantities of this treasure, had been a bookkeeper in his grandfather's whiskey distillery.

"Old Overholt" people called his grandfather, and that was the name of the whiskey too. Although the business was a well established and thriving one, Frick's pay was very small. He earned only a thousand dollars a year.

But, as Carnegie had said, Frick was ambitious. He had no idea of spending his life as his grandfather's bookkeeper. He saved as much money as he could and borrowed more. He began to buy up the land under which the rich veins of bituminous coal lay. Quietly he added more and more to his holdings. He talked to no one, and no one seemed to realize that old Mr. Overholt's bookkeeper was accumulating holdings in the bituminous country.

When the panic of 1873 forced many small farm mortgages to be foreclosed, Frick was ready to borrow more money and buy up the farms under whose fields lay the precious bituminous coal. After a while he went to a banker and offered the land he had bought as security against a large loan. He wanted to build five coke ovens in Connellsville, Pennsylvania, for the Connellsville region yielded a particularly good coking coal and Frick knew that if he could get a corner on the Connellsville market he could drive out charcoal from the steel-making industry.

This was the young man whom Carnegie spoke of that day in the woods at Cresson—a young man of "great ability and great energy." Frick agreed to the proposal that he should join Carnegie's company.

It was not hard to see that the union of the world's greatest coke producer with the world's greatest steel producer was a happy one. Specially constructed ore vessels were bringing what seemed to be endless amounts of iron ore from the Lake Superior ore mines through the Great Lakes. From here it was transported by rail to Pittsburgh. The coke which Frick could supply seemed almost without limit. The blast furnaces were ready to work day and night making iron for Carnegie's steel mills, and he could find a market for all the steel he could supply.

Frick was a hard worker and ambitious. Before long he had become executive head of the Carnegie Steel Company. He took care of the company's production and established its labor policies. Gradually he was given more and more responsibility.

By 1886 Andrew Carnegie's mother and his brother Tom had both died. Then it was that he married and spent more and more of his time in Scotland, where he had bought a big estate which he called Skibo Castle.

The birth of his little girl, whom he and his wife named Margaret after his mother, gave him extraordinary happiness. His letters home were filled with her sayings and doings.

Meantime in America steel production grew by leaps and bounds. The wooden shacks where the steel workers lived went climbing up the hillsides outside the company's plant at Homestead, Pennsylvania. Hungarians, Poles,

Italians, Czechs and men of many other tongues crowded the entrance of the steel works when the morning whistle blew. Carnegie had a kindly attitude toward these European peasants who worked in his mill. He wanted them to be well treated, though he was absolutely opposed to having them organize into unions.

In the summer of 1892, Carnegie was at Skibo Castle, and the labor policies of the Carnegie Steel Company were in the hands of Henry Clay Frick.

Frick, for all his industry and energy, was a cold man. When the steel workers came to him to say that they had organized a union, he discharged them, built a high fence around the works and announced that he would employ only non-union labor.

The steel workers' union was not to be stopped so easily. If Frick and his managers were to shut themselves up in their stockades, the union would prevent new workers from coming to the plant by blocking the road. Angered, Frick sent for a company of armed Pinkerton detectives to help him. The union men saw them coming down the river on a barge. They fired on them, and the Pinkerton men returned their fire. Then there was terror in Homestead, both behind the steel company's stockade and in the streets of the town. The governor of Pennsylvania sent the state militia to restore order. When the conflict had finally been quieted, it was found that three of the Pinkerton men had been critically wounded and five of the steel workers were dead.

The news of the Homestead strike blazed in great newspaper headlines across the country. Many people upheld Frick's action in hiring his armed police force, for America had not then come to understand the point of view of organized labor. But there were many also who deplored the kind of war that had been carried on at Homestead.

Meantime. at Skibo Castle, Andrew Carnegie was saddened by news of the Homestead strike. It weighed on him heavily, for although he was a fierce business competitor, he was fond of his men and often paid them tributes for his success. This is borne out by the fact that, after he retired to devote himself to philanthropy, his first gift was to his workers. He set aside $4,000,000 to establish the Andrew Carnegie Relief Fund, which was to be used in compensation for accidents, and for pensions.

So now when the news of the Homestead strike was brought to him, he was deeply distressed. It was not that he himself would have recognized the union, but Frick should have found some better way of dealing with the men. If *he* had only been there, things would have turned out differently, he was sure of it.

There was a long series of disagreements between Carnegie and Frick after that, and finally Frick resigned from the company.

21

MR. SCHWAB MAKES A SPEECH

On the night of December 12, 1900, a line of horse-drawn carriages crowded the gas-lit street outside the University Club in New York.

"Good evening, sir! Good evening, sir!" The doorman greeted the arrivals who looked strangely alike in fur-lined overcoats and tall silk hats. Eighty of the most important bankers in America had come to dinner.

The dinner was given by Edward J. Simmons and Charles Edward Smith. It was in honor of Charles M. Schwab, president of the Carnegie Steel Company, who had shown them hospitality the preceding year. Not a single important banker was missing that evening, and the prince of them all, J. Pierpont Morgan, was seated at the left of Mr. Schwab.

Who was this "Charlie" Schwab to whom the bankers paid such honor that evening? He was the same man that Carnegie had chosen to replace Captain Bill Jones some time before. A big, jovial, red-faced man whose deep laughter resounded under the flow of restrained conversation—a man the bankers knew only slightly, an important man whom some of them wanted to know better.

After the dinner was over—oysters, clear soup, fish, squab, a sweet, and the customary wines in their customary parade of glasses—when the coffee cups and the brandy glasses were scattered across the table and the blue haze of the fine cigars rose above the bankers' heads—then there were speeches. And Charles M. Schwab made a speech.

"There is only one thing I can talk about," he began. "It is the only thing I know anything about—that's steel."

He had begun a half dozen speeches in exactly that way, but since no one there that night had heard any of them it did not matter.

Charles M. Schwab had come a very long way before he stood facing the assembled bankers that night in 1900. He had been born of German parentage in the little town of Loretto, Pennsylvania, which is near Johnstown. As a boy he had sometimes climbed up to a hillside near the town to look across a valley toward Johnstown. He liked to watch the smokestacks and the plumes of smoke above the foundry chimneys, and the glow of red when some furnace door was left open. "And the murk was always present," he said afterward "—the smell of a foundry. It gets into your hair, your clothes, even your blood."

He had driven a stagecoach for his father when he was eighteen. But he was not content to stay at this. One day he went to Captain Bill Jones at the Homestead steel works and asked for a job.

"Can you drive piles?" Bill Jones asked him.

"I can drive anything," Schwab had answered.

So he was hired to drive piles at one dollar a day.

His progress was quick and brilliant. He rose like a rocket, someone said. Before long he was chief engineer at the Braddock works. Then he was superintendent of the Homestead Mill, and finally, perhaps because his interest in metallurgy and mathematics combined to make his reports so clear as to attract Carnegie's attention, he was made president of the Carnegie Steel Company.

So now tonight he stood before the assembled bankers and talked of steel.

First, he painted a vivid picture of the prosperity of Carnegie's steel mills. He showed that whatever profits were made had been turned back into the company. Thus, when expensive improvements were needed, there was always plenty of money. Whenever equipment was out of date, it was scrapped at once and replaced with something of a newer type, he said. Recently many of the Bessemer converters had been replaced by the new open hearth furnaces which produced steel in much larger quantities than ever before.

The bankers puffed gently at their cigars. They liked to hear of expensive equipment and large sums of money being spent.

"But Carnegie's genius does not stop

there," the enthusiastic Schwab went on to say. "He is not content to have the largest and best-equipped steel mill in the country. He wants to control also all the materials he needs to make steel. He has bought up large numbers of ore mines and coke ovens. And he has bought shipping lines on the Great Lakes and railroad lines that feed in and out of Pittsburgh. They are all in his hands—he has integrated them all."

Integrated? The bankers were interested in the word. Carnegie was a genius, the bankers agreed. That was how a great industry was brought into being.

But Schwab's speech was not finished. "There could be an even greater integration," he was saying.

Then he began to lay before the men at the dinner table a plan so vast in its scope that every one of them was dazzled by it.

"The whole steel industry ought to be completely reorganized," he announced. They had not expected this kind of speech. But he continued:

"It's not economical to have one plant produce half a dozen steel products as they do now. Production ought to be planned so that one mill produces the steel rails, another the steel plates and still another the steel beams. They would work twice as efficiently that way, but there would have to be some single body to do the overall planning.

"And another thing that ought to be planned is the location of the various mills. They have been built here and there, in a haphazard way, with no thought of the markets they will supply or the cost of transportation to those markets. Why, nearly a third of the price of steel is taken up in transportation costs. Re-establishing the mills in the right locations would certainly bring down the price of steel. But there again you would need joint ownership and overall planning."

His audience was listening now with the greatest attention. Perhaps, after all, there was something in what he said. Schwab paused a moment, looking around the table.

"Integration like that I have suggested would certainly make the steel industry prosper. It would make all America prosper. . . . But what company would have capital enough to undertake such integration? There is not a single steel company that is rich enough," he said.

Beside him J. Pierpont Morgan puffed steadily at his expensive cigar.

The dinner was over. The guests rose to leave. Morgan asked Schwab if he could talk with him. There were some points he did not understand.

Did Carnegie know that Schwab was making that speech? He had not come to the dinner although he had been invited. He never spoke of it afterward. But for many years he had talked of selling out his steel interests. He had said long ago that it was a disgrace to die rich. "Men should retire from active business at or before sixty," he had written.

Was Carnegie pulling the strings that night when Charles M. Schwab made his speech? Nobody knows. But he was sixty-five, well past the retiring age that he had set himself. If he wanted to retire, certainly this was the opportunity.

"Do you think Carnegie would sell out?" someone asked.

After that there was a meeting in the luxurious library of the Morgan house. John W. Gates was there and Roger Bacon, who was a friend of Theodore Roosevelt, and Schwab, who had brought a brief case filled with reports and statistics, as well as Morgan himself. The four men talked all night. It was snowing heavily outside when they began, they remembered, but it had cleared sometime before midnight. The sun was streaming in at the windows before they had finished.

At last Morgan pushed back his chair and rose to his feet.

"Well," he said to Schwab, "if Andy wants to sell, I'll buy. Go find his price."

But did Andy want to sell? Schwab decided that he would question Mrs. Carnegie about it first.

"Why don't you take him out for a round of golf?" she counseled.

Schwab and Carnegie played at the St. Andrew's Club near Yonkers on the outskirts of New York City, and afterward they lunched together and Schwab told him of Morgan's wish to buy.

Carnegie listened quietly. Morgan, who controlled more money than any other man in the United States (than any other man in the world, perhaps), was offering to buy his business, to integrate it with the other important steel companies. He was asking him to name a price. It should be a moment of triumph, and he knew it. But suddenly he was reluctant. Could he part with all this that he had built up through an active life?

"Let me take the night to think it over," he said.

He was in better spirits when he met Schwab next day. He had made up his mind. They talked of figures and terms. Then he drew a pad toward him and took up a pencil and wrote down a figure.

"That's what I'll sell for," he said as he pushed the pad toward Schwab. The figure was $400,000,000.

It was thus that the United States Steel Corporation was born.

Carnegie called on the great banker a few days later.

"Now, Pierpont, I am the happiest man in the world," he said. "I have unloaded this burden on your back, and I am off to Europe to play."

And Morgan, who was usually gruff and had

little to say, put down his cigar for a moment to shake him by the hand.

"Mr. Carnegie, I want to congratulate you on being the richest man in the world."

The two men met again not many months later on the deck of a steamer that was taking them to Europe.

"Pierpont," Carnegie said to the banker, "I made one mistake. I should have charged you $100,000,000 more than I did for that steel business."

"If you had," Morgan answered, "I would have paid it."

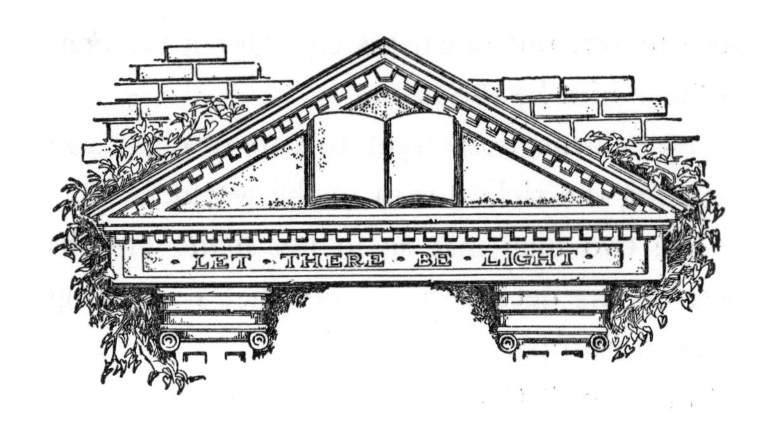

22

WHAT SHALL A MAN DO WITH HIS MONEY?

By the time he was ready to sell out his business to J. Pierpont Morgan, Andrew Carnegie had accumulated a huge fortune. Perhaps he himself did not know exactly how much it amounted to. But he had always believed that the money did not really belong to him, that he was only the "trustee" of all this wealth.

"He said he should consider it disgraceful to die a rich man," wrote his friend William Gladstone, the English prime minister.

But how ought Carnegie to dispose of the wealth he had accumulated? What could he do with it?

At Skibo Castle in the Highlands of Scotland where he had been staying at the time of the Homestead strike, Andrew Carnegie pondered this question. He found Skibo Castle a good place for thinking. It was very elaborate with crenelated towers of pink and white stone, well reinforced with steel that had been rolled in Pittsburgh. A great park lay around it and there were green lawns and massive plane trees. And the air was soft with the fragrance of rhododendrons that bloomed even in January. There were lakes and streams on the estate that were good for fishing, and moors for grouse hunting, as well as golf courses, and a swimming pool whose water, brought in from the North Sea, was electrically warmed. Over the castle a bright flag fluttered. It was made of an American flag and a British Union Jack sewed together face to face. Carnegie felt that both countries were his, though he had become an American citizen.

To Skibo Castle Carnegie brought his friends. They awoke in the morning to the sound of bagpipes and breakfasted gaily to the strains of organ music. They could fish and shoot and swim and play golf, or sit and talk. Carnegie himself took part in all these things except the shooting, and enjoyed particularly his daily swims and his little yachting trips on the nearby firth.

"I am so busy working at fun!" he wrote a friend. "Fishing, yachting, golfing. Skibo never so delightful; all so quiet! A home at last."

Yet all the while, as he walked on the moors with his favorite dog Lassie, or sat among the birches and the bracken looking out at some distant view, he was thinking not only of the business of fun but of the responsibility of the fortune he had accumulated.

"Of every thousand dollars spent in so-called charity today, it is probable $900 is unwisely spent; so spent, indeed, as to produce the many evils which it proposes to mitigate or cure," he had once written in an article called "Wealth" in the *North American Review.*

How could he avoid this waste of the fortune he had been able to accumulate? He wanted, not to give charity, but to wipe out the causes that made men vicious or ineffective. Ignorance, he thought, was what blocked all progress. To do away with ignorance was the new trade he embarked upon.

The free public library was the greatest instrument for doing away with ignorance, Carnegie believed. The library at Dunfermline, for which his mother had laid the corner-stone, had been one of his first public gifts.

Now he would give buildings for other libraries and encourage communities to match his gifts with books.

Soon his secretaries, both at Skibo and at his house in Ninety-first Street, were busy with applications for library grants. And Carnegie dreamed that thus he might be able to place a book in the hand of every man, woman and child in the United States. Only about a third of the libraries he gave bore his name, but over the door of most of them an open book was carved with the words, "Let There Be Light."

"I am now giving away libraries at the rate of two or three a day," he wrote exultantly to his friends.

For over twenty years he carried on this library campaign. In 1919 it was reported that he had built 2,811 libraries valued at over $60,-000,000. Of these libraries 1,946 were in the United States, and the rest in Canada, Great Britain and other English-speaking places.

Some of them were in far-off spots like Tasmania, New Zealand and the Fiji Islands.

Carnegie was supremely happy in doing this work. He said that he liked to imagine "the tired and weary worker" with a book "which arouses his imagination, carries him into enchanted regions, shows him pictures that dazzle, leads him through palaces surpassing those of Aladdin, and gives him a world to revel in, far removed from the world of his daily toil and cares."

But there were other uses for his wealth besides the libraries that he loved so much. His friend, Sir Arthur Balfour, had written, "It is to science that we have to turn for the future of the race," and when he considered it, Carnegie believed that this was true. At the beginning of the twentieth century people were saying that the preceding hundred years had disclosed more of nature's secrets than the five thousand that had gone before.

Andrew Carnegie determined to add still

more to that knowledge. He would build a great scientific institution—the Carnegie Institution in Washington, D.C. Its purpose according to its charter was "To encourage in the broadest and most liberal manner investigation, research and discovery and the application of knowledge to improve mankind."

The Carnegie Institution which he founded had a staff of gifted scientists bent on uncovering nature's secrets. They studied the past and the future of the earth—the evidence of the land bridge that had once linked North America and Asia by way of the Aleutian Islands; the gigantic rift between Africa and Palestine; the formation of the coral islands in Samoa and the Tortugas; the origins of earthquakes; the floating meadows of diatoms, minute living organisms in the sea.

They tried to find out why whales, which had lived on the land for many generations, had taken up their abode in the ocean. They tried to find out how green plants absorb their energy from the sun. They sent a wooden ship, the *Carnegie,* whose planks were riveted with copper nails, to study the errors that magnetic compasses made. Even the buttons on the sailors' suits in this vessel were made of bone instead of metal. There must be no iron anywhere about the ship if scientists were to have a better understanding of magnetism. They studied the case histories of five thousand families to learn more about heredity, and established the first nutrition laboratory in the country in order to get a better idea of the relation of food to health.

Carnegie thought the Institution's greatest achievement was in astronomy. On a high cloudless mountain in California the Institution built the Mount Wilson Observatory. There the scientists set in place the 100-inch telescope by which they could penetrate into the far reaches of space. Here they saw the spiral nebulae receding from the Milky Way at incredible speed out into the unexplored limits of the universe.

Once in the evening at Skibo Castle, Carnegie and his friends looked at lantern slides taken at Mount Wilson. "I must go there," Carnegie said. "I must see these things before I die."

Then he gave another $10,000,000 to the Carnegie Institution, and he wrote a letter:

"I hope the work at Mount Wilson will be vigorously pushed, because I am so anxious to hear the expected results from it. I should like to be satisfied before I depart that we are going to repay to the old land some part of the debt we owe them by revealing more clearly than ever to them the new heavens."

There were other benefactions besides the libraries and the gifts to pure science. Carnegie made a gift of $4,000,000 to Dunfermline. "It's the most sacred spot on earth to me!" he said. The letter that accompanied the gift began:

"Gentlemen of the Commission,

"The trust deed of which this may be considered explanatory, transfers to you Pittencrieff Park and Glen, and $2,500,000 in 5% bonds . . . all to be used in attempts to bring into the monotonous lives of the toiling masses of Dunfermline more of sweetness and light; to give them—especially the young—some charm, some happiness, some elevating conditions of life which residence elsewhere would have denied; that the child of my native town, looking back in after years, however far from home it may have roamed, will feel that simply by virtue of being such, life has been made happier and better."

He was not less generous to Pittsburgh than he had been to Dunfermline, for he gave the city, besides its library, a concert hall, an art gallery and museum, and an endowment to maintain them.

"Pittsburgh is the smokiest place in the world," he wrote Lord Balfour. "It has never been anything but a center for materialism; has never had a fine hall for music, nor a museum, nor an art gallery, or public library, and yet the result proves that there has been lying dormant the capacity to enjoy all these."

Still his desire to distribute more and more wealth was unsatisfied. Carnegie gave endowments to small Scottish universities, to technical schools in America, to small struggling colleges.

"Can you tell me how I can spend $5,000,000 or $10,000,000 to the best advantage? I shall give a prize for the best answer," he wrote a group of American leaders.

He gave at least 8,000 organs to churches of various denominations and established a Hero Fund for the recognition of civilian heroes. Then he established a foundation to provide pensions for retired professors, and gave money for a Peace Palace and international law library at the Hague in Holland. After that he created an endowment for studying the causes and prevention of war.

In 1911 Carnegie realized that his capital was increasing and not diminishing. His wealth was growing faster than he could spend it. He hated to think that when he died his wife would be burdened with it. He therefore established the Carnegie Corporation, an organization to which he gave the rest of his fortune for distribution, reserving only about ten per cent of it for himself.

The last ten years of his life were happily spent in reading letters from old friends. Many of them were in need—the girl who had held his school books for him while he went sliding in Dunfermline, two sisters with whom he liked to dance when he was a young fellow, a boy who had been a messenger with him in the early days at the telegraph office in Pittsburgh, and dozens of others. He gave annuities to all these people, remembering his youth and trying to repay everyone who had been kind to him.

His list of benefactions grew longer and longer as time passed. He gave grants of $25, $50 or $100 a month to old poets, scholars and novelists. In this way he distributed about $250,000 a year to some 409 persons. And he set up a trust fund of $4,250,000 to make sure that these annuities would continue after his death. "My monthly pension list," he called it. (There was no such thing as social security then.) Later, in his will, he created an additional trust fund of $6,282,000 to pay annuities to some 45 people designated in his will.

So the little blue-eyed man in the tweed suit grew older, and who can say that this was not as happy a time as any in his life? He loved to think of the money he had distributed.

"How much did you say I had given away, Poynton?" he asked his secretary.

And Poynton, who was a very accurate fellow, answered, "$324,657,399."

"Good heavens," Carnegie replied then with a chuckle, "where did I ever get all that money?"

23

AIR CASTLES FALLING

"It can't be true. . . . Are you sure it's true? Can't America do something to stop it?"

Andrew Carnegie was pacing up and down the library at Skibo Castle. It was the summer of 1914.

Carnegie's old friend, Robert L. Ritchie,

who was the minister of the Scottish parish, had come to Skibo that morning with bad news. Great Britain was at war with Germany —or would be within a few hours. Her allies would soon be involved, and the conflagration would certainly spread to all Europe. There was not much doubt that America would join.

Andrew Carnegie heard the news with incredulity. "He was a very distracted man," Mr. Ritchie said later, remembering how Mr. Carnegie had paced the floor at Skibo.

"All my air castles have fallen about me like a house of cards," Carnegie said.

True, in the last few years he had built a great many air castles and made a hundred schemes that concerned themselves with peace. The longer he lived the more intense became his love for human beings and for the ancient earth. The destruction that war brought seemed to him unbearable.

"International war is the foulest blot on our

civilization," he wrote. "We still kill each other like barbarians." And again, "It decides not in favor of the right, but of the strong."

Carnegie had done all he could in the cause of peace. He had gone to visit the German Kaiser in an effort to persuade him to reduce his armaments. He had written long letters to the British Prime Minister. He had talked to Theodore Roosevelt, to Taft and to Woodrow Wilson, and had written more letters to them.

But he had not stopped with talk and with writing. He had given substantially of his wealth in the same cause. The sumptuous Peace Palace at the Hague in Holland had been built with his money. It housed a Court of International Justice and an extensive library of books on international law. Again, he had transferred $10,000,000 in United States Steel bonds to establish an Endowment for International Peace, whose trustees, men distinguished in law, education, science and public life, "were pledged to hasten the abolition of international war, the foulest blot on our civilization."

He had been working at another idea—a plan for what he called a League for Peace. He wanted a formal alliance of the great nations, which should be reinforced by an international court and an armed force. Such a League, he thought, if he could only persuade the nations to join it, might establish the peace of the world.

"But all my air castles have fallen about me like a house of cards," he said again, pacing up and down the castle at Skibo that summer morning in 1914.

The Carnegies sailed for America on the *Mauretania* in September and did not see Skibo Castle again. Carnegie offered his great house to the British Government, hoping that they might use it as a hospital for wounded soldiers. It did not prove suitable, however, so it was closed. The forests in the great park were for the most part cut down because the government was in need of wood.

Back in his house on Ninety-first Street in New York City, Carnegie sought to carry on his life in a world at war. He had now given away most of his great fortune, having kept only enough to provide for his wife and daughter, and to live in comfort.

Sometimes he drove out to St. Andrew's Golf Course in Westchester County for a round of golf with some friends; sometimes he walked around the reservoir in Central Park. But he missed the heather-covered hills of Skibo, and he missed his dog Lassie. He read newspapers and magazines and wrote letters. In the quiet evenings he played backgammon with Mrs. Carnegie. And all the time, behind the scene of this quiet life, he knew that men were killing each other in the muddy trenches they had dug in Europe. This he had been unable to prevent.

In 1915 Carnegie had a severe attack of grippe, from which he was very slow in recovering. When finally he was able to be up again, he seemed to have lost a good deal of his vitality. Now he no longer walked in the park or played golf at St. Andrew's. Mrs. Carnegie wrote most of his letters for him.

The garden which lay beside his house on Ninety-first Street was still a source of happiness to him. People walking along the street used to look in through the tall iron fence to see where he was sitting in the shade of a tree or strolling along the border. He nearly always wore a piece of lemon verbena in his buttonhole.

Two happy events occurred in those last years: a visit from his Cousin Dod who came from Dunfermline to see him, and the marriage of his daughter Margaret.

Because the Scotsman who had been reared in the cool misty climate of the north could never stand the summer heat, and because it was impossible to get to Skibo now, the Carnegies bought a beautiful house, called Shadowbrook, in the Berkshire hills of Massachusetts. It was there on August 11, 1919, that Andrew Carnegie died.

It is sad that the steel master's last days were darkened by the thought that he had failed to bring peace to the world. He had probably accomplished much more than he realized. International law had become a real force in the world through the work of the International Court of Arbitration at the Hague. The association of nations which he envisaged did come into being in a somewhat different way in the League of Nations. And when the League of Nations was destroyed, the idea persisted and took new form in the United Nations.

And besides all this, thinking men have continued to work steadily and persistently for peace. They have written books, pamphlets and magazine articles; they have lectured at schools, colleges and public forums. They have not succeeded in doing away with war, but they have kept the bright prospect of peace before men's eyes. And much of this has been made possible through the generosity of the weaver's son from Dunfermline. The air castles which Carnegie said were falling around his head are not all in ruins. Some of them have very strong foundations.

24

THE AGE OF STEEL

Andrew Carnegie was buried on a hill in Sleepy Hollow Cemetery at Tarrytown, New York. It had been only seventy-one years since the day he stood on the deck of the sailing ship, looking at New York City and wondering what America would be like.

America had changed since that day—and he had had a hand in changing it.

When he first saw them, the little cities on the eastern seaboard were built of brick and wood. Horse-drawn carts and carriages rattled along the poorly paved streets. There was no running water.

Further west, back from the coast, the cities were smaller; and then, as you journeyed on, there were no cities and no great farms. There America was a land of forests and of waving grass. Buffalo grazed on the untenanted plains, and there were roaming tribes of Indians. The adventurous in that day crossed the continent in covered wagons, seeking furs, or gold, or richer fields of wheat and corn.

But in the seventy-one years since the Carnegies landed in New York, the cities had been crowded with people from Europe. Locomotives went shrieking across the plains on tracks of steel and crossed the rivers and canyons on steel bridges. Steel tractors plowed the fields, steel farm machinery reaped and bound the ripened grain. Steel made the pipes that carried water to irrigate the crops. Steel made the wire that fenced the farmers' fields and bound in the herds. Steel made the mine shafts that reached down into the earth. Steel reinforced the concrete dams that controlled the flow of water in a hundred rivers.

In the factories wheels turned night and day to produce the objects made of steel: the pins and needles, the tools and guns, the pipes and wires and steam shovels; the bridge parts, boiler plates and ship plates; the high-speed transmissions and gears for automobiles, busses and aircraft; the strong girders supporting structures of glass and metal—the towers of the new cities.

Andrew Carnegie, lying on his hilltop at Sleepy Hollow, had not himself brought all these things to pass, for it needs the labor of many men to change a continent. But it was Andrew Carnegie, more than any other person, who had brought about this new age in America—the Age of Steel.

INDEX

Index